the VIRGIN STONES

For more information visit:
www.virginstones.info

© Joyce Withers 2003

All rights reserved
Published by Temple Design, 23 New Mount St, Manchester.

Printed and bound in UK by Biddles Limited

ISBN: 0-9543956-0-3

the VIRGIN STONES

a series of spiritual insights

Joyce Withers

For Gaia

CONTENTS

CHAPTER 1
Awakening / 1

CHAPTER 2
A Hole in the Whole / 4

CHAPTER 3
A Hidden Language Code / 11

CHAPTER 4
The Human Connection / 26

CHAPTER 5
Blowing in the Wind / 34

CHAPTER 6
The Virgin Stones / 52

CHAPTER 7
A Reflection of Another Dimension / 73

Conclusion / 80

Notes / 89

Glossary / 94

Bibliography / 98

About the Author / 100

Author's Note

This book explores a series of spiritual insights. It is less concerned with traditional knowledge than with intuitive, heartfelt knowing.

Whatever you may think of these ideas, whether you feel that they are true or just a figment of an active imagination, the likelihood is that you will not forget them. They may change the way we think about ourselves, the people around us and the planet we call home.

For me, the intensity of the original experience which brought them to me has faded now, leaving the essence of something very precious and ancient. The panorama of knowledge that I touched is still there, I'm sure, just outside the boundaries of our ordinary consciousness, just beyond our reach. To have been there was a privilege, whatever the consequences of my expedition.

Like a traveller who returns from a journey to the remotest region of the planet, the urge to share the experience and to describe what we have seen is a strong one. Our heart may be full to overflowing with the sights, sounds, light and colour of where we have been, but when we try to recapture it, to share it with our friends back home, it loses so much in the telling. Our language leaves us weary and disappointed when we try to use it for a task that is beyond its capacity. We eventually fall silent to avoid the strain of applying such a blunt instrument to such a sacred task.

The greatest loss for me is not found in the recounting of the finer details or even in the huge pieces of esoteric knowledge that I feel sure I have left behind somewhere. Perhaps these are things I was never meant to recall, perhaps some things are truly impossible to translate into this physical reality. I don't know.

If I could change anything, it would be to bring back to this place and time the experience of deep unconditional love that surrounded me and permeated all of my being during part of the period when these insights were given. It will never be forgotten. To share it with everyone would mean so much more than whatever else is offered here. All I can hope is that the depth of that love somehow weaves itself into the writing here and helps to illuminate the truth – and that its echo will always stay in my heart.

The ideas described here did not necessarily arrive in the order in which they are written, nor were they all received at exactly the same time. I think that the nucleus of each one sprang into my consciousness at some time in 1984.

The earth is embryonic in nature – a living organism of which we are an integral part. We have a hidden energy system in common and in understanding our own spiritual component, we can begin to understand the subtle energy system of the planet on which we live.

Human beings were part of the original creation process and continue to be creators within the system. This is a unique position and carries direct responsibility for the future. Human genetics are instrumental in balancing some mechanisms of the planetary whole.

Wind and water (Feng Shui) are one of the means of transmission of information between human beings and the consciousness of the earth.

Within the English language and landscape are hidden *markers* or *pointers* to another higher spiritual reality. When we understand our unique position in the scheme of things, and start to look at ourselves as spiritual beings on a human journey, we can begin to identify them.

Some people have reincarnated here for millions of years to hold the balance and structure of the living organism we call Earth. Their presence is indicated in the monument we know as Stonehenge and is reflected in similar stone circles and standing stones everywhere.

Our present physical reality is a *reflection* of another spiritual level of consciousness. Call it heaven, nirvana or whatever name we like. It exists alongside this physical world and everything we know here is an expression of it in some way. There are some very practical examples of those reflections given here.

Each of these insights or propositions could provide enough material for a book in its own right. They can be expanded upon endlessly. Each should be read and considered independently of all the others because, while I have tried to make the connections necessary to bring them together, they were originally given to me individually. It may be that the links I have suggested are mistaken ones and this might distort the meaning of the original material.

So, this is my attempt to record something special, something which I feel could be important. It is written as simply and honestly as I could do it.

Joyce Withers
Manchester, England
Spring 2002

Acknowledgements

In writing these pages it was important to express only the insights which arrived with me in 1984 and which have since been built upon and expanded by my travels and studies. The ideas here came in several bursts of enlightened knowing and understanding during a spiritual awakening all those years ago. It has taken all of those years to consolidate that knowledge and then to have the time and space to express it in such a way that others might share these insights.

Along the way, since 1984, I have listened, read, travelled, taught and tried to learn different ways of expressing this knowledge. There are those whose work I have encountered which closely reflected my own insights and I would like to acknowledge this and to thank them for their significant contribution to the expansion of understanding in this subject area. (This is not to say that any of those named below would necessarily agree with the contents of these pages or of my attempt to express this knowledge, complete with any of my own mistakes in interpretation.)

Firstly, to Helena P. Blavatsky whose life and work was dedicated to bringing esoteric knowledge and Eastern philosophy into the public arena in the nineteenth century. I feel her description of the *virgins* (Kumaras) in *The Secret Doctrine* (first published 1888, Theosophical Publishing House) greatly reinforced my original insight and eventually provided the confirmation of this esoteric knowledge I had been searching for. I am aware that the creation process she describes in *The Secret Doctrine* is very similar to that which I have tried to express here and it was a great relief to me to read her words, which arrived in my personal library in the late 1980s. I am not sure if her virgins are the same as mine, but I suspect it may be so.

To Douglas Baker, founder of Claregate College, London where I studied from 1986 to 1990 by correspondence. The explosion of knowledge which was mine in 1984 created an urgent need in me to find a way of structuring the information. My background was not an academic one, nor had I studied these subjects before, so I was rather at a loss to know where go to find the tools I needed to work with this material. My thanks to Peter W. of Manchester Metaphysical Society for my introduction to Claregate College at that time. The structured nature of the course was exactly what was needed. Dr. Baker's many publications cover a wide area of metaphysical studies but I am especially grateful for the information contained in *The Jewel in the Lotus*, (Baker, 1975) and *Meditation – The Theory and Practice*, (Baker, 1975), giving a simplified view of the Chakra energy system also to be found in *The Chakras* by C. W. Leadbeater, (Quest, 1927) and the huge amount of information contained in the books by Alice A. Bailey (Lucis Trust). Thanks also to Edith G. for my introduction to the White Eagle teachings at that time and her long friendship.

To Dr. Peter McNiven and all the staff at John Rylands Library, Deansgate, Manchester for their encouragement and help in searching for and finding so many volumes during my years of research there. Having an alcove in such a magnificent atmosphere and setting certainly gave me every encouragement to work on material which may well have proved tedious in other circumstances.

The period spent in research and retreat at The Theosophical Institute at Krotona in California was a significant one. As well as giving me time and space to read *The Secret Doctrine* again and to survive my first real experience of speaking in public, this was where my original article *A Hole in the Whole* was written (*Theosophical Journal*, July/Aug 1994 Vol.35 No.4). My thanks go to Joy Mills and especially to Nancy and Roger Elsinger for their kindness and encouragement, and to Barbara T. for her help and long friendship. Also to Ianthe Hoskins at the Theosophical Society in England for her support at that time, and members of the Theosophical Society at Bolton for their quiet encouragement.

Other authors whose work has reflected some of the ideas contained in these pages are listed below. I cannot entirely express the feeling of pure joy that leaps into my heart when I open a book and discover – perhaps in just a few lines in one chapter – something which reinforces the insights which are expressed here, or even provides another piece of the jigsaw puzzle. So my gratitude and thanks must go to:

Dr. Richard Gerber for *Vibrational Medicine,* (Bear & Co, 1988) which I carried home with me from the USA in 1990. It has been a vital part of my library since that time.

William Bloom for all of his work but especially *Money, Heart and Mind,* (Arkana/Penguin 1996).

Dr. Serena Roney-Dougal for her pioneering work in parapsychology and *Where Science and Magic Meet,* (Element, 1991). The achievement of her PhD. in parapsychology, which was mentioned at her lecture in York in 1994, was a great incentive to me. I began studies for my B.A.(Hons) that same year.

Robert M Hoffstein, *A Mystical Key to the English Language,* (Destiny, 1992) for showing many other possibilities within this language. Also David Oates of Reverse Speech Technologies for his fascinating and much needed research into the speech patterns found – especially within music – when lyrics are played in reverse.

Jacques Benveniste for his courageous research and attempt to expand the boundaries of conventional science regarding *the memory in water*.

Elizabeth Clare Prophet and The Summit Lighthouse for their information and teachings found on the internet (http://www.tsl.org/teachings).

To Zachary F. Lansdowne for *Rules for Spiritual Initiation,* (Weiser, 1990) which helps to simplify and explain the human initiatory experience which is mentioned here and discussed more fully in the Bailey books.

And finally to Brian Raymond whose excellent drawings helped me to illustrate and explain many of the ideas contained here (while his contribution does not necessarily imply any agreement or acceptance of these insights).

To the very many other authors past and present who have written in metaphysics, parapsychology, spirituality and healing, and to New Age writers everywhere, including those whose material is channelled from another source. All have contributed to the great spiritual expansion of knowledge which is taking place as the Age of Pisces, which was one of *belief*, gives way to the great Age of Aquarius which is one of *knowledge*.

Their efforts have created a climate in which these insights can now be explored and openly discussed.

SPECIAL THANKS

To R. & S. without whose help and support the original draft would not have been written. To R.A.B. for showing me it was fine to think differently all those years ago. To A. for his constant encouragement and interest. To P. for her light and laughter, and to G. for his trust in me and my book. Finally, to B. for her considerable editorial skills and to N. for his help in checking the manuscript.

Thanks also for the peace of the farm on the bay, where some parts of the book were written.

To all who have supported my efforts since 1984 on different occasions and in so many places along the way. They will know who they are.

If we want to understand something new, first we must begin to evoke the ancient memory of it in our heart.

We start to awake our already-knowing inner self or soul.

CHAPTER ONE

Awakening

This series of insights came in a traumatic upheaval of spiritual awakening in 1984. Other pieces of the puzzle have arrived since then, occasionally as a result of reading, listening and sharing with others. Most often they arrived in those quiet times of personal isolation and aloneness.

The ideas are offered in the spirit in which they came – as a series of insights which leave each of us free to accept or reject according to our own truth. In spiritual knowledge especially, we never teach or learn anything which is entirely original. If we want to understand something new, first we begin to evoke the ancient memory of it in our heart. We awake our already-knowing inner self or soul.

In August 1984, I spent a hot, sunny afternoon at Liverpool Garden Festival. It was the time of the drought and there had been no rain for many weeks. We wandered among the flowers in the early evening and I remember standing against a metal guard rail, looking out over the Mersey, across the waters of Liverpool Bay. A huge bank of dark cloud began moving inland, silhouetted against the clear blue sky and we reluctantly decided to make our way back to the car just as it started to rain. The clouds moved across the sun and suddenly it became very dark and ominous. It began to rain heavily. I had this feeling of urgency, at first just associated with the storm. But the feeling continued after we reached the car and on the way home. The music of Liverpool, and especially The Beatles seemed to surround me and fill my mind. Later, I felt that I had become aware of the song *Lucy in the Sky with Diamonds* as though the music were somehow being impressed on my mind. The feeling was so strong that when we reached home, I went straight from the car into the lounge and over to the record cabinet. I remember staring intently at *Sergeant Pepper's* album sleeve for a long time. The impression simply would not go away and remained with me for a long time.

A few days later I was lying in bed early one morning. A warm summer breeze drifted through the open bedroom window and the venetian blind swayed gently, reflecting the morning sunlight into the room. I was almost awake when I felt a great warmth and tenderness surrounding me. It was a wonderful secure, loving feeling and I opened my eyes and gazed around the room which was bathed in early morning light. Resting quietly on my pillows, surrounded by the warmth, I began to sense that something was about to happen. It began with that urgent feeling once again.

The picture which filled my mind was so brilliant, so clear and beautiful that I sat straight up on the bed and gasped in amazement. 'It's an embryo', I whispered, hardly daring to speak in case it disappeared, 'this planet – earth – *it's an embryo.*'

The impact of something so vital and so incredibly beautiful is indescribable.

What followed was a raising of my consciousness in a way I find impossible to explain. For many years I have felt that this failure to describe these events was mainly down to my own inadequacy in communication, but finally I realise that what I experienced was a totally non-verbal phenomenon. It was mind-blowing, as though I were suddenly connected to all knowledge, but on an entirely different level – an *intuitive* one, I think. Some of the insights arrived at that time, although I had no way of expressing them or even beginning to understand the full implications of the knowledge.

Unfortunately, no one around me at that time understood what was happening to me and neither did I. The experience lasted several weeks with other, more traumatic events following. The result was horrendous at the time, with some incredible long-term consequences. It changed my life completely.

The only other occurrence of any real relevance to these pages happened in the days immediately following my visit to Liverpool.

I was unable to sleep and sitting alone in the living room of my home. Someone called my name, clearly, in the quiet hours of the night. It happened suddenly, as though a radio had been switched on for a few seconds only and a male voice said my name – *Joyce Withers*. This is my maiden name but at that time I was married and had not used that surname for sixteen years.

I did not hear anything else, nor have I heard anything similar since that time. I was startled rather than afraid and while the tone of the voice was totally expressionless, I was left with the feeling that something was now required of me.

Everything that followed served only to reinforce this understanding, and so began the journey along the road I still travel today.

CHAPTER TWO

A Hole in the Whole

In the beginning we were. We are part of the original creation process and our essence is that of the creator. Our genetic pattern has formed a template for other life forms here and we are a vital part of the evolutionary process of the whole planet, not just passengers on spaceship earth.

We have *always* been. Earth is embryonic in nature and we were instrumental in the original creative process on this planet. Now we have arrived at a point in planetary evolution where we have a choice whether to begin to understand and accept our unique position, or to abdicate in favour of the popular belief that humans evolved entirely by chance from another animal species.

That viewpoint is certainly more comfortable, because it allows us to misunderstand the real reason for our being here and, in doing so, we then fail to accept our responsibility for what follows in the evolutionary process. We defer to the idea of the survival of the fittest, forgetting the real meaning of the *fittest* in the grand universal picture.

In reality, the choice here is ours and the consequences of what we choose will be ours to live with forever. We were there in the first magnificent burst of energy and power into the universe and our position in the scheme of things was encoded into our unique DNA patterns.

On the physical level Earth could be viewed as a closed system. All that is required to sustain life is encapsulated within the planetary atmosphere and everything that happens inside here is contained within that whole. This observation is about to be fully understood by ourselves with the impact of global warming and the greenhouse effect.

The biological and scientific causes of these events are well documented and researched. The ideas and suggestions contained in these pages try to give another perspective, one which is best appreciated by those who have explored and understood the hidden alternative view of mankind. This is most usually found in metaphysics and other alternatives including healing, complementary medicine and holistic science. The foundation for these metaphysical concepts is contained in the teachings and writings of the early Theosophists of the nineteenth century. Their significant contribution to New Age thought should not be underestimated.

The depletion of the protective ozone layer surrounding this planet is, by any consideration, a serious event with life changing, if not life-threatening, consequences. However, there could well be other possibilities for these planetary changes and other, less obvious, implications.

To understand what these are, it is helpful to have some knowledge of the subtle energies which surround and interpenetrate the human body and the greater 'body' of the planet itself. Only then can we begin to understand the creative process of which we, as human beings, are an integral component.

Prana or Chi, the energising life force in nature, flows through the subtle bodies of the human being and interpenetrates the physical one using the channels known as meridians. The subtle energy body forms a matrix which allows this energy to circulate, and this is intrinsically linked to the greater subtle energy field of the planet itself.

Once this is understood, it becomes obvious that the actions and health of each individual human being will have a direct effect on the planet and the reverse will also be true. Changes which occur within this system will have a direct effect upon ourselves and all other life forms here.

In healing (therapeutic touch) there is usually a flow of pranic energy from healer to patient. The healer may be particularly sensitive to any changes in the aura of the patient and can often feel places around the body where the subtle energy field is different in some way. This might be interpreted by the healer as hot or cold, uneven or smooth or, most significantly, as a thinning in the wall of subtle energy surrounding the person. The change detected may not necessarily be in the area of the injury or disease, but could show up in other places, perhaps following one of the meridians used in acupuncture.

Sometimes the condition is quite severe and the healer can detect actual holes in the aura.

In the same way that our physical body suffers damage from accidents and injuries, the fine web of the energy-body reacts in a similar way, especially to turbulent thought patterns and strong emotions. There are other external influences, such as pollution, radiation and electromagnetic fields. It is important to bear in mind how the physical body and energy-body interact and to understand how any change in one will inevitably affect the other. The idea now held by some doctors and most complementary practitioners, that disease begins on levels other than the physical level, can perhaps be illustrated here.

Disease is sometimes better understood as *dis-ease* or an inability to be *fully at ease and connected with our real inner self*.

The consequences of such a misalignment are expressed in different ways – everything from tiredness and mild mental depression to life threatening physical illness such as cancer. If mental stress and emotional disturbance impact on the subtle energy-body before the effect shows in physical illness, then it follows that if we can detect changes in the personal energy-field, this information will be useful as a diagnostic tool, helping prevent physical illness developing later. Similarly, some accidental injuries and infectious illnesses with more immediate onset (such as influenza and other viruses) would then impact eventually in the individual subtle energy field. It is possible that in the not-so-distant future technology will build on the advances made with Kirlian photography, bio-feedback and similar techniques. Then we will be able to see such impacts on our subtle energy-body more clearly.

Smoking and alcohol have a coarsening effect on the energy-body and will reduce its high frequency level and compromise its efficiency. They are sometimes unconsciously used by us to deaden our sensitivity to unacceptable elements in our lifestyle or surroundings. They make it possible, often at the expense of our health, to live or work in circumstances which would otherwise be intolerable to us. (Consuming meat and other animal products will produce similar effects and similar consequences for some people.)

The influence of these substances is felt most acutely when an attempt to change is being made. Giving up smoking, alcohol or perhaps becoming vegetarian almost always involves a period of intense personal adjustment. The stress of making such a change cannot be underestimated. It is one of the main reasons why failure to break these existing patterns of living is so common.

The sudden increase in sensitivity as the subtle energy body becomes revitalised and begins to vibrate on a much higher frequency is unexpected and little understood. The resulting stress often makes the transition period unbearable.

However, giving up tobacco and other substances before real damage has occurred is one thing. Dealing with the consequences of the disease process is another.

What we experience on an individual human level can apply on a planetary scale too.

The hole in the protective ozone layer surrounding Earth is the result of a dis-ease process within the planetary whole, caused by changes made by ourselves, some of which produced widespread pollution and resulted in a serious imbalance within the system. The consequences on more subtle, higher frequencies may now become apparent as the planet strives to make the necessary adjustments for survival.

THE HUMAN SUBTLE ENERGY-BODY

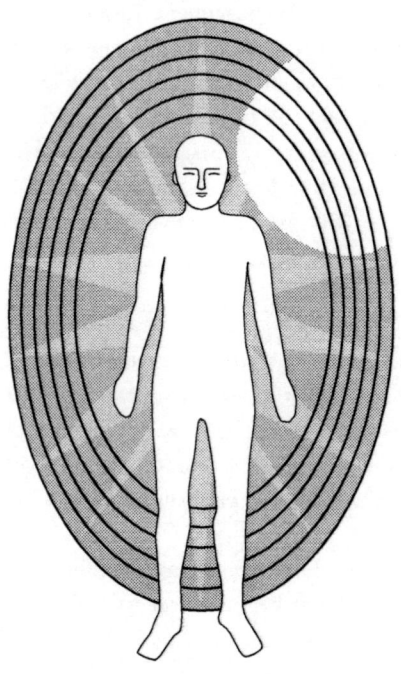

An impression of the human subtle energy body which includes an area where the energies appear depleted, giving the impression of a hole in the surrounding energy field.

The Planet's Subtle Energy-body

The same impression of a subtle energy body, but this time of the planet. This suggests a similar area where the subtle energies have been depleted, perhaps eventually resulting in an actual hole in the physical atmosphere surrounding the earth.

Rather like the changes in the human subtle energy field when dis-ease is present, the planetary subtle energy field is retracting and becoming thinner in an attempt to allow more *chi* energy from the sun to penetrate. In doing so, it also allows ultra-violet radiation to flood the planet. *This is similar to the treatment by radiation of cancer in humans.*

Could it be that we are about to receive a dose of our own medicine?

Bear in mind the time scale involved is far greater for the planet than for an individual human being. If we injure ourselves the shock and pain are felt almost immediately, but for the huge planetary system in which we live, the time between the event and the resulting traumatic response is far longer. Many years may pass before the result can be registered and by this time the connection between the cause and the effect has been missed by us.

The scientific causes of the *hole in the whole* are still the subject of investigation and this is not intended to challenge any possible conclusions, but rather to give another less obvious and more rarely understood perspective. These ideas are intuitive in nature, based around a system of knowledge long hidden from the everyday world, but rather more familiar to those who have studied the mystery teachings.

CHAPTER THREE

A Hidden Language Code

Only when we begin to understand who we really are can we start to observe another reality in the world surrounding us. We can even glimpse our life pattern not in terms of one short time on Earth, but as millions of years of existence, many spent within this particular planetary environment. We start to change the way we perceive our world and our own personal reality.

When our personal picture changes, so do the criteria upon which we base our decisions and judgements. That is important, not just for ourselves and our own immediate environment, but for the planetary whole. We may not already be aware of the impact our individual choices make in the overall scheme of things and these pages could hold some surprises for many of us.

Those of us who were here when the planetary creation process began were polarised into a particular structured pattern, a network of energy points rather like the acupuncture points on the human meridians.

The pattern was not the same for everyone, some points on the planetary web were major centres for the transmission of information and energy and those who held these positions were chosen especially for their personal qualities and unique abilities.

Some points, where it was very important to maintain a balance, were allocated to *twin souls* or *primary soul-mates*, as these individuals have a natural inclination to reflect or mirror the qualities and achievements of each other. This happens between these souls even when great distances separate them and whether or not they are aware of each other's existence. This would explain the way in which similar ideas and cultures emerged in different places across the planet.

MERIDIANS

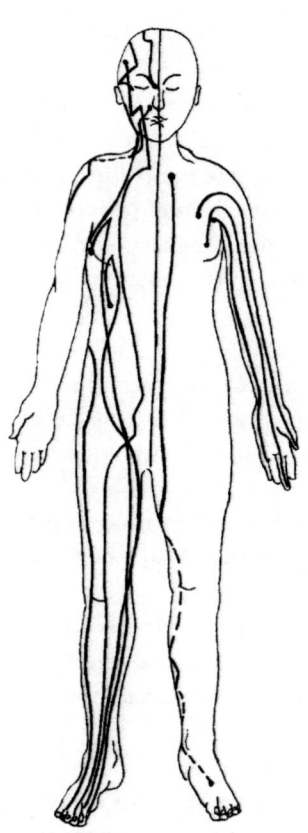

Some of the energy channels (meridians) used in acupunture. Fine needles can be inserted at known points along these channels to stimulate the subtle energy flow.

There are others who incarnate in a pattern of *triangular* energy. This is often where three (or sometimes more) aspects of the same soul energy incarnate for a special purpose. The picture I visualise is similar to the arrangement of Bucky Balls – a recently discovered carbon atomic structure and also of the ozone molecule when seen clairvoyantly (*Occult Chemistry,* Besant & Leadbeater 1951, 3rd edition). In view of the current environmental crisis surrounding the thinning of the ozone layer in the atmosphere, this observation could be significant.

The triad is a very stable energy pattern and one which, like the balancing mechanism of the twin or primary soul energies, is still repeated today throughout the world. Those souls who incarnate as a triad are often less aware of their connection to each other than twin/primary souls (although twin/primary souls can themselves also be part of a triad, the one may not exclude the other).

Most societies encourage relationships producing energy patterns which bring people together in couples and this subtle programming makes it more difficult for souls who are part of a different pattern to accept their status, even though their relationship with each other may not have any sexual component. Indeed, some souls who are part of one of these energy patterns may never meet at all. In some incarnations, when a triangular configuration does arrive together in order to do a piece of progressive or evolutionary work in the world, it is one of the most successful group combinations. It is also one of the most emotionally painful and difficult energy patterns to live within. The individuals concerned feel pulled between two different directions and this friction can be emotionally draining as well as also providing the impetus for intensive learning and soul progression. This is particularly difficult when the triads are linked together, one member of each triad forming part of another group, in what can be an extended configuration.

CLAIRVOYANT VIEW OF OZONE MOLECULE

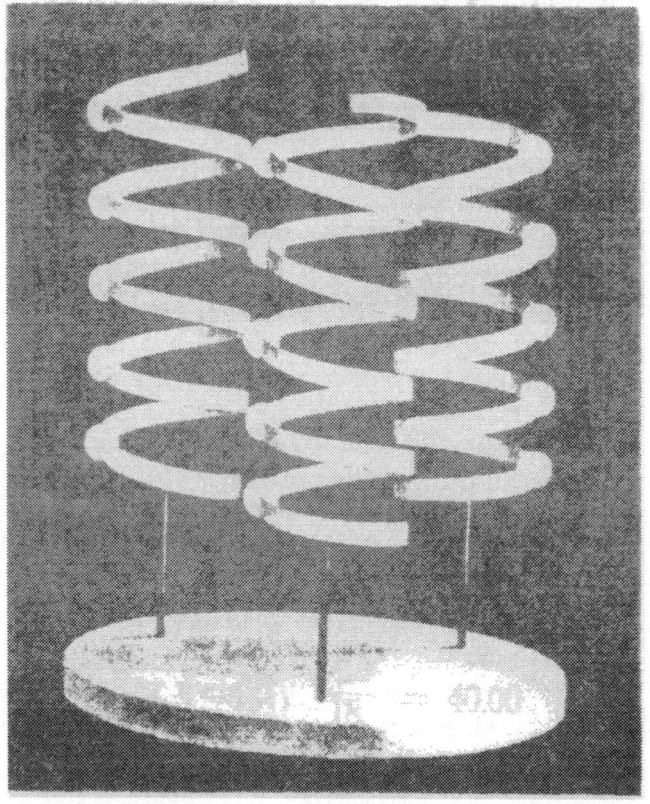

OZONE

'The appearance of Ozone is indicated in Fig. 47. It is composed of three Oxygen snakes, that is, of one Oxygen atom of two snakes, and a third extra snake of half Oxygen. These three snakes are at the points of an equilateral triangle. They are on one plane, so that as they revolve, the large bodies within each snake come together at the nodes. Ozone being thus 1 / 2 (0), it is found that there are two varieties of Ozone. Fig. 47 shows one variety made of two positive snakes and one negative. The second variety of Ozone is composed of two negative snakes and one positive...'

(Photograph and text reproduced with the kind permission of The Theosophical Publishing House)

The configuration extends to include the *square* or *quadruple* pattern which is especially dynamic.

There are many different group patterns and combinations, from twin or primary souls (or twin flames, which constitutes the final configuration, when those whose origins were together return to each other), triangular groups, groups of four, right up to and including the special configuration of the *sacred circle* of global initiates working across the world. All configurations, including those of initiates, can and do include other patterns within them.

The original communication between our spiritual selves during the primal creation process was intuitive and non-verbal. It flowed most easily between the individuals who are linked in one or other of these groups. However, as the creative process and distances increased, and the planetary environment became progressively more densely physical, this communication changed gradually into the physical phenomenon we now hear as sound.

This sound was the primal music of this sphere and it formed the basis for our current language. This was the original 'Word' referred to at the beginning of St. John's gospel.

What was once a delicate, intuitive and non-verbal transmission between the creative spiritual beings of the past (ourselves) has now become the audible verbal language of the present. Language has moved along beside us, from the original highly spiritual state to a now much lower physical existence and will move back again, as we evolve towards the higher frequencies once again – on another loop of the spiral of existence.

Verbal communication is far more complex than it first appears. The language we use today works on at least three levels:

The first level is the ordinary speech we use to communicate each day throughout our lives.

The third level is one of pure sound. On this level the meaning of each word or phrase is irrelevant, rather the tone and undulation of the sound is what matters. We can glimpse a little of this idea by simply listening to someone speaking in another language where we cannot interpret the meaning. What we actually hear is just a flow of sound. If we listen imaginatively, it can seem that the intonation of the speech reflects the qualities of the land from which the speaker originates. A predominantly flat landscape – like Finland – can produce a rather monotonous tone, whereas the hills and valleys of Wales tend towards a tone which is undulating. We can almost imagine the changing Welsh landscape when we listen to the native language because the rise and fall of the hills and valleys is somehow encapsulated in the sound of the language. Perhaps the striking, often rugged landscape of Scotland is also reflected into some of the local dialects.

In between these two levels of speech or sound is another more coded and complex layer.

The idea that some words and sounds simply live within the language as a *marker* or an *unconscious key* to another level of thought is almost magical. This inspirational insight into the second language level is essentially one which comes with the opening of the human heart centre, or heart chakra.

It seems that the energies needed to access this level of thought are essentially love-based and, as such, are most easily available to those who have begun to develop these universal – unconditional – love qualities within themselves. Their energy-body has evolved to the point where it is open to receiving these energies and they are, in effect, initiates of a greater planetary awareness. They are beginning to love unconditionally.

Some words have evolved within our language that have a direct connection with our higher spiritual existence and also give clues to the way in which our presence here controls and affects the whole environment. We have taken these words for granted, but sometimes the most effective way of concealing something important is to make it blend into our everyday lives. Then, when someone suggests there is something special or mystical about an otherwise ordinary expression, it seems silly. *The best way of hiding anything important is to make it seem ridiculous.*

The *ear* is our instrument for receiving sound, for hearing. It is also part of the word *earth*, implying another ear or mechanism for receiving vibration or sound. Our *heart* has this hidden *ear* in its centre and the *hearth*, which has long been considered to be the centre of the home, also conceals this hidden ear within its sound. There are so many other words that link to this sound-word such as fear, tear, dear, gear, near, rear, year and, of course, the *ear* of corn. The element most closely connected to sound is the *air* element.

Could the sound or vibration carried on the wind be recognised by the planetary consciousness in some way – like a musical code, giving information needed for survival and evolution? All grain (g-rain = g = geo + rain = earth-rain) needs water to flourish and the rains are carried in cloud formations which are wind-dependent. The suggestion is that information of a type of which we are as yet unaware is carried on the wind and originates from us – from words, sounds, music – and from the higher frequencies it can detect within our energy bodies. The energy body or aura (aura = vital air or breath in Sanskrit) itself is a product of our own self, our total well-being and our genetic inheritance. Its subtle vibration produces our own individual note or song.

Interestingly, genetically modified corn produces shorter stems and bigger cobs and is therefore less susceptible to wind damage. Might it also behave differently as a conductor for the vibrational energy carried by the wind? If a different note or sound is produced – even slightly different – will that make any significant change to a hidden mechanism which could be important to the way in which grain is produced? Perhaps on some level this planet is consciously aware of a need to balance the production of plant growth in order to sustain life, which in turn is its own creative life force.

If this whole idea sounds really bizarre perhaps we should remember that sometimes within the most improbable of ideas lies the key to something wonderful, and often it just needs someone to grasp that key and give it a turn.

What is important is that we are sure of exactly what we are doing before we introduce an artificial change into the agricultural matrix that cannot easily be removed.

At the time of writing an area of genetically modified crops twice the size of the United Kingdom has been planted in the last few years world-wide. One different note can change the structure and meaning of the whole song.

Sometimes the sound of a particular word can give a clue to its true meaning, even though we have learned to write and to spell it differently, like *rain* and *reign*. One is the life-giving water that our crops depend on to grow and the other is the life-time of the monarch, who might have been originally chosen for his/her responsibility for the harvest and prosperity of the people. *Monarch* could be interpreted as *Moon-arch* meaning the *arch of the moon* which could also describe a position within the ancient stone circles. The title would indicate his/her place in the circle of individuals who are represented by the standing stones. Perhaps this was designed to ensure that the balance of energies was right within the circle and that, in turn, could help to produce a good harvest.

The genetic component is important as this was the means of transmission of the *frequency* or *vibration* needed for this unique position. This was because the flow of energies across the land was conducted through these vital energy points or earth chakras by the *light* or *ley*-lines.

Even the word king can express this connection i.e. Kin-g = *kin* meaning *related* to, then the letter 'g' there to represent the earth or soil, as in *geo*. The similarity between the words reign and rain is significant because *it is the sound of the word* that matters, not the way we spell it. Even the word *coronation* implies a *corona* – a halo – which is now represented by a jewelled crown.

The understanding which comes as our intuitive spiritual nature begins to unfold is again based on the original concepts of sound, frequency or vibration.

There is a hidden sound within the word grain. If we take the letter *g* here to relate to *geo* or earth, then the connection between grain and rain is made, grain = earth-rain. There are many more of these verbal insights and it is possible, once we have the key to these markers in the English language, to begin to connect them to the physical markers in the English countryside.

Time is an intriguing word. The sound has tie as the emphasis and can break down as *ti-me*. (This is the interpretation of someone who hates to be tied to time in the conventional sense.) Perhaps, because time itself has a unique presence on dense physical levels of existence (but becomes irrelevant on higher levels), there is a similar connection lurking within the human psyche. The idea that the word time can express within it a spiritual impression of being tied here is a fascinating one. It is essentially suggestive of a strong binding hold on the individual.

Then there is the word *love*. It is a gentle but strong sound.

The real nature and meaning of this word is still there, even though misused and often abused during the last century. The energies here are circular and inclusive – this is reflected in the main vowel *o*. Whenever the letter v appears in a prominent position within a word, it can link that word with the impression of *descending spiritual energies*. The shape of the letter gives that idea. Love then translates as a gentle, strong energy, circular in nature, descending from a higher level of consciousness. The word then becomes an expression of *lo* or *low* joined to v (also associated with the planet Venus, which is understood to be the alter-ego of Earth in astrological terms and known for its connection with love energies). Therefore the word love becomes *an earthly expression of descending higher spiritual energies*.

The idea that our present language developed from a collection of animal sounds, punctuated by an occasional expressive grunt, is about as misplaced as our conviction of an ape-like ancestry (although our spiritual energies may well have 'en-souled' a particular animal species in order to allow these high frequency energies to descend further into physical matter).

On the contrary, our use of language today is a reflection (into our physical world) of a highly spiritual communication-flow which has *always* existed on higher levels. The language we use and understand each day is a poor substitute and only a faint reflection of the real communication which was originally possible between us. This real communication often still takes place sub-consciously between members of the same soul group, where the love-based subtle energy links continue to allow the flow of information to happen.

Originally, within the energy-body, and on a frequency above that of the physical level, our communication was instantaneous and essentially non-verbal. It consisted of relayed impressions of thoughts and energy – similar to that of our present emotions – giving much greater freedom of expression and accuracy of description. Telepathy and other forms of E.S.P. (extra-sensory perception) are ways in which we can consciously begin to experience that energy flow today in some individuals.

Our musicians, poets and artists try with varying degrees of success to recapture this original perfect form of expression. This higher level of communication was functioning during and after the original creation process and it still remains, its markers barely echoing within our language. It is a mechanism which is rarely glimpsed from our normal verbal perspective, but it is there operating within our daily speech patterns. When we begin to appreciate that our language was originally a purely spiritual communication, we can begin to recognise the signposts and markers within it. This particularly applies to commerce and finance, which is another hidden energy system.

The word *currency* usually means money. Money which we have received in exchange for work, and the work we do requires a release of physical energy – even if we are just sitting using a computer keyboard. The word *current* can also mean a flow of electricity (energy) and again, *current* can mean *at the present time or now*.

Currents occur in water, and water is very often found near a ley line or other subtle energy centre, such as a stone circle. A current is itself a stream of fast-flowing water, which can also be flowing underground.

In England the pound is presently a unit of currency. The word pound is also used to indicate an enclosure or fenced area or even a prison. This is a place where someone (or something) is held securely. The word can also mean to beat or to hit repeatedly as in the way a drum is beaten – a means of creating sound.

When we bring all these ideas together we can have a rhythmic beating (pound-ing) of a drum or similar instrument, in a safe or secure enclosed area (a pound) and perhaps producing – or celebrating – a current or energy/water flow. The drum is considered to be a sacred instrument by the indigenous peoples of North and South America, Africa and some parts of Europe including the Arctic regions. It has been used in shamanic practices world-wide. Sound travels most easily through water.

Also, the word *money* itself can be interpreted as *moon-eye*. The *eye* (or light) of the moon?

The link is really tenuous and vague. This is only the faintest remnant of something which is buried in our modern language, something which may have had its roots in pure sound on another, purely spiritual, level of existence. The language we use today can only find the weakest links to that reality, links which have survived for millions of years buried within our psyche.

The word *electricity* is similarly fascinating. Whenever *el* occurs at the beginning of a word there is usually a highly spiritual connection. *El* is another way of expressing *the most high* (Allah or God) and there is always a strong spiritual component to the word it fronts. Elhoim, elevate, elder, Elvis (!), elect and elate are all examples of words with raised energies which are fronted by the *el*. So the word *electricity* can be broken into meaningful syllables as follows: *el* being from a higher spiritual source, *elect* being ones who are specially chosen and prepared for something (initiates), *tri* meaning three in number as in triple or triangle – perhaps a triad-soul configuration – and then the word *city* ends the sequence. This would perhaps indicate a *seat* or *site* or some fixed position although today it means a place where many thousands of people live together and often have done so for a long period of time. The two meanings are not entirely unrelated.

Stonehenge is a circle of stones linked together in a triad pattern with other sets of three stones within the inner circle. *This arrangement is an illustration of the original 'power network' always existing between the connected triad-souls of the individuals in the hidden circle.* It was based on sound.

In the circle at Stonehenge, the stones with higher frequency vibratory levels are now understood to be concentrated in the centre of the circle, and those with lower frequencies are on the outside. Recent research has shown that those stones in the centre give a completely different set of frequency readings when exposed to the same sounds. There is a real correlation between this and the different levels of human initiation. This is explored in the chapter entitled The Virgin Stones.

The ancient Egyptian word for the human energy-body is *ka*. The Egyptian ka was a spiritual body or *vehicle* for operating on higher levels of consciousness. This name is also used to describe the soul of a king after death. Then we have our word for a physical vehicle here today – car. Two different words, from different times and cultures both with the same sound and both expressing the idea of a vehicle.

The pathways or power lines necessary to encourage the fast, effective communication or movement of our spiritual ka were the original energy channels, within the energy-body of the planet. They were there long before the physical evolution of the earth, whose particles formed around their original creative pattern. Although it is possible for the ka to travel anywhere (rather like an off-road vehicle) its natural passage is along one of these energy-lines which serve in this instance as our roads do. These special lines not only connect the energy centres here on earth, they have planetary connections too. This is the reason for the special alignments of structures like the pyramids and Stonehenge. They are connected to a much wider network which is inter-planetary.

(It is possible that the lightening in electrical storms somehow follows the energy channels in the surrounding subtle energy field of the planet.)

Our cars and transport system are a modern reflection *in dense physical terms* of another much older system which continues in existence today, but on another, higher level. Even the word *highway* seems to suggest a *higher way*. The words *road* and *rode* have another deeper but tenuous link. Bearing in mind the correlation between our roads and the network of light-lines described earlier, then the spiritual meaning of the *horse and rider* can emerge. The horse usually represents the *understanding* while the rider represents the *intelligence*. So the road/rode connection can express a link to another level of spiritual understanding.

Once again, an abstract idea has been incorporated into our everyday language.

When we lost touch with the higher frequencies many thousands of years ago, we still held the subconscious memory of life on those levels, even after the lines of light or ley lines had almost disappeared. We still recognised their intersections and major junctions, which are similar to the subtle energy centres in our bodies, as significant sacred places (sacr = light) and continued to erect heavy stones to mark and to magnify their energy presence. These are the dolmen and stone circles found throughout the countryside. Churches now occupy some of these original sites. They arrived much later, sometimes built on top of a prehistoric sacred area, which in itself may have recalled an ancient memory of the original creative process which depended on its stations or communication centres.

These potent energy points were held only by certain evolved individuals who could be entrusted to withstand the very intense energies found at intersections on the universal grid. The initiation process, while hidden from our general awareness, is a process currently engaging many human beings on earth today. It ensures that only those who are capable of doing this work will find themselves drawn to live on those points. Today, this could be within a city, town or village in just an ordinary street, where one particular house is centred on a vital, hidden, energy point. The individual who lives there might have had to withstand severe trials over many lifetimes to ensure that he/she is tuned to the energies involved and well prepared to withstand them. These concerns are rarely, if ever, known to that individual who may simply feel drawn to a particular place or area where they feel happy and at ease (because their particular energies are compatible with the location) and then create a home there, sometimes finding it extremely difficult ever to leave that particular place.

Many of our ancient fire festivals took place on specially significant sites, and perhaps we can draw a parallel between the lighting of those fires at sacred sites and the use of moxibustion techniques in acupuncture. Both can stimulate the energy-flow along a particular channel, one in the human body and another in the planet.

Human beings do that too, when they live on particular energy points where their unique vibratory note can stimulate and harmonise, so encouraging and assisting the subtle energies of the planetary system to flow. Almost always this takes place unknowingly and most individuals will live out their lives without ever being aware of the effect they have within this subtle energy network.

CHAPTER FOUR

The Human Connection

This insight carries the most difficult, confusing, and ultimately interesting picture – the way it came to me was also strange and less than clear. It is included here because to leave it out would be dishonest, as I have tried to make this an accurate record of the insights which were given to me. The picture that was shown to me was of the generations of peoples, but as a song like a great musical evolutionary pageant or procession, each human being carrying their own note or song onwards to be expressed into the music of this particular sphere.

How was this note or song encoded into our being? Do we unconsciously know which note we have been chosen to play? These were questions that troubled and confused me because although the idea of the song was clear, the *voice* of the individual singer was somehow muffled.

Then one day, standing in the queue at the local supermarket, I patiently watched as the checkout operator processed the purchases of the person ahead of me in the queue. The customer was hurriedly packing items from her shopping trolley. Every now and again the operator would pause as she came to an item where the bar-code had been covered by a special offer label with a lower price. These items had to be charged separately and the bleep of the checkout machine was temporarily silent.

Like most people, I hate waiting in queues. However, the huge advance in retail technology which bar-codes provide allows the checkout operator simply to pass the item across the desk where a hidden detector recognises the code and generates the correct price for the item. This is so much easier and quicker than having to look at the price tag and key in the amount for each purchase, as it was in the past. The bar-code is a great innovation.

To the retailer the bar-code means much more than a quicker way of getting customers through the checkout. It allows purchases to be recorded and stock levels to be maintained. The bar-code is part of a monitoring system, a way of knowing which items are in the store and of choosing which product lines to re-stock.

The way the vertical black lines of the bar-code are arranged identifies each item individually and gives specific coded information about that particular item, such as the name of the product, weight, size, and of course, the price.

This could be rather like the genetic code in human beings. Our genetic code is a collection of information which, when arranged in a particular way, makes us who we are – it provides our unique identity pattern.

Eventually, when read by someone with a good understanding of the coded biological information, it can tell them a lot about who we are too. We can identify the purpose and significance of each gene, with the infinite possibilities to medicine and society as a whole that this idea suggests. If we can identify genes which cause disease then we have the possibility of repairing or replacing them.

While most of us have reservations about the use of genetic engineering, the possibility of a world where only healthy babies are born is certainly an attractive proposition to many people, and one which we may be fast approaching.

If we are part of an evolutionary process which allows for the survival of the fittest, then the question must arise as to why our own reproductive mechanism has failed to adapt to allow us to screen out — on a genetic level — all human embryos which do not have the potential to develop into perfect human beings. Why does this screening not already happen automatically, so that the only viable embryos are those which will develop into perfect humans? Many pregnancies do, in fact, result in miscarriage in their early stages and this has been accepted as a natural mechanism designed to eliminate foetuses which are not viable, only allowing human reproduction to progress when the chances of a satisfactory result are higher. This mechanism has not allowed us to screen out all hereditary disease naturally.

If it is possible to manipulate the genetic structure to eliminate those genes which carry hereditary disease, then — if this is a good idea — why does our own evolutionary process not do this already? It has served us well — as far as our survival is concerned — for millions of years. If the evolutionary process depends on the survival of the fittest then why, within the human genetic structure, does material remain which has the potential for producing disease? *Perhaps what the evolutionary process considers to be the fittest does not exactly match what we consider to be a perfect human being.*

It may be that our evolution has reached a point where further progression is entirely dependent on our intellectual and scientific ability to make deliberate changes to our own genetic structure. We can now make those adjustments using our intellectual and scientific skills because, at this stage in our existence, that is the next rung on the evolutionary ladder. Or is it *necessary* for us to carry the hereditary characteristics which are continually transmitted into our gene pool, even if they appear less than perfect to us? *They could fulfil a purpose within the planetary whole of which we are as yet totally unaware, and, by making what may seem to be logical and caring choices in genetic engineering, we could be missing something crucial to our survival.*

Our future depends on knowing who we are and what our real function and purpose is here. We were part of the creation process and are now the caretakers of life on this planet.

Our decision-making process currently depends on a practical, scientific world view which can only give us a glimpse of the total reality of our true position in the real scheme of things. It is based almost entirely on the view that human beings are intelligent animals with a limited life span who utilise the planetary environment for the comfort and survival of themselves and their offspring.

For most of us this view, although sometimes tempered with a personal belief system based around one of the major world religions or some other spiritual component, is enough to define our position in the world. Often, our current thinking depends on the idea that we are descended from some other related species and have evolved into who we are through that evolutionary pathway.

But if we were part of the creation process and we are still here, then we are almost certainly part of the maintenance programme on this planet.

If we are part of the organic or natural evolutionary processes of this planet, then perhaps we need to be – genetically – just as we are. The planetary organism or consciousness within which we live will automatically generate the human components it needs for survival and to fulfil the original purpose. If that is true, then the consequences of making changes within our own genetic patterns would leave us in a difficult if not dangerous position from an evolutionary perspective.

Our presence here is mandatory, not accidental. The responsibility for the future of this planet and everything living upon it is ours in ways in which most of us have not yet even dreamed.

Back at the supermarket, the bar-code monitors stock levels of each particular item. When one line of goods is selling well stock levels will decrease and, at a certain point – triggered by the bar-code – re-ordering from the wholesaler or manufacturer will be requested.

Is it just possible that this happens in some way within our human world population? To view humanity in this way may seem callous and uncaring. Most people would agree that to compare us to a can of peas or a frozen chicken from the supermarket is inappropriate at least. Here we are not comparing like with like, rather we are looking at a possible mechanism operating within this planet, one which has been hidden from our perception for millions of years. The comparison with the supermarket bar-code is just a convenient one which might help to illustrate the idea. It is certainly not intended to view human beings as a commodity, rather to try to illuminate an elusive mechanism, which when fully understood might help to give us another perspective on our lives within this planetary system.

Human beings bring a unique vibratory pattern to each incarnation which is linked to their D.N.A. code and it is essential that the right balance of human energies are incarnate here at any one time. This works at a sexual level too, generating the right balance of male to female human beings able to reproduce, who are incarnate at any one time. If we need to have a particular number of individuals with the potential for specific gifts and skills then there has to be a way of monitoring and serving those needs. This requirement would have been there from the beginning, then expressed in the arrangement of particular individuals and soul groups because of the qualities they brought to the creative process.

Bearing in mind that our tendency is to recreate here on earth a reflection of what already exists on a higher level, perhaps what we have created in the bar-code process is a reflection of another mechanism linked to our D.N.A. code.

A bizarre suggestion, of course, but one which if we accept the possibility – for just a moment – can lead us on to other possibilities.

There must be, within the human genetic code, a mechanism which triggers other processes within the planet – perhaps controlling environmental influences which we had previously believed to be simply forces of nature, such as wind, rain and global climate.

If we are the creators and maintainers here and we have so far been unaware of our responsibility, then this has to be an automatic process. This, in turn, means that there is a hidden mechanism in operation which has been there – like ourselves – from the beginning. The suggestion is that the D.N.A. present in every human cell is vital to the planetary evolutionary process because the material it contains is an integral part of this process – **it is the human bar-code**.

Somehow this code is recognised within the consciousness of the earth and is intrinsically linked to the environmental and ecological processes of the planetary whole, and, like the bar-code, the genetic code carries a *best before* or *expiry* date.

Every individual song must eventually come to a natural end and another way of exploring this strange bar-code idea is to go back to the *sound* or *frequency* viewpoint or perspective.

The earth as a sphere vibrates at a unique frequency. This is the planetary note and everything within the planetary sphere – including ourselves – combines to produce that particular frequency. Each individual on this planet brings his or her own unique vibratory note to the whole, and this serves to enhance the overall sound or song. Rather like the players in an orchestra, everyone donates their particular note to the whole planetary song. It is interesting that the leader of an orchestra is called a *conductor* and this word is also used to describe something which allows electrical current to flow.

Imagine sprinkling a handful of sand evenly over the skin of a drum. We can think of the sand just as tiny particles of matter, scattered at random over the whole area of the drum skin. Then gently begin to beat the drum. The sand forms itself into a pattern, responding to this vibration. The beat changes slightly and so does the pattern it creates in the sand.

If we are represented by the grains of sand on the drum skin, then our collective frequency or vibration changes slightly as new notes and rhythms arrive with each generation and are modified with each birth or death. Some phrases, chords or individual notes repeat themselves again and again, forming the main theme of the song. The beat goes on.

The word universe literally means one song. The earth is the *ear-th*, which again suggests an ear or something which receives those sound waves.

When we look at the human genetic code perhaps we are glimpsing something of the original music score. It is then a most crucial component in the structure and pattern for the whole evolutionary process.

Just like the bar-code, the genetic pattern of each individual will determine whether he is part of the essential background of the music or different in some way, perhaps to be born when unique gifts or skills are needed to enhance the song.

This hidden mechanism produces the right people at the right time, that is, it produces whatever is needed to progress the evolutionary process in ourselves and in the earth itself. Its other hidden purpose is to stimulate the biological impulses within the planetary whole which provide the means to produce enough to feed everyone. This is a hidden balance operating on our planet which we have not yet understood.

The genetic connection is expressed here in what I hope is an intuitive and sensitive way.

The correspondence between the genetic code and the bar code is given simply as an illustration. However, if we can accept that many of the systems we have created here, such as our transport system and our monetary system are based on something which already exists on a much higher spiritual level, then this comparison can take its place alongside the others.

This particular insight has always been a difficult one for me to grasp and to express. I feel that sometimes we are given the best tools available to us and the feeling of recognition that came to me with the bar-code comparison was a strong one.

This is not science-based research. It is an attempt to open a door of intuitive perception which has been closed to us for many thousands of years. Once again, these ideas can only be really appreciated from the perspective of our eternal presence here and from within the shift of consciousness that this new understanding brings.

My hope is that I have expressed this idea sensitively and accurately enough to allow others to glimpse something more of the view through this secret door.

CHAPTER FIVE

Blowing in the Wind

Many people living on this planet are permanently on the verge of starvation. The political and racial issues which prevent everyone here from having enough food to eat are complex. They have little to do with the natural mechanisms of the planet which are geared to provide about the right amount of produce to feed the human beings and animals alive at that time. *Human population and food production are intrinsically linked.*

It is possible that rituals involving human sacrifice in some parts of the world may have been connected to the hidden knowledge that there was a link between the components of human blood – the D.N.A. or the bar-code – and fertility in the plant kingdom. The genetic connection was once accepted and understood, its secret guarded by those who sought to protect something vital to the evolutionary process.

The problem with closely guarded secrets is that they tend to get lost or distorted when passed down through the generations. Often all that remains is the ritual and ceremony which once served a real practical purpose. Without the original knowledge, the ritual and ceremonial events become a meaningless empty echo of something which was once so important.

The priesthood of ancient Egypt, South America and other ancient civilisations were aware of the connection between the human component and the harvest. The *ears* of wheat often placed in tombs and coffins in their ancient burial traditions were not simply intended to accompany the deceased as a food item for passage into another world as we have understood. The corn and ears of wheat were placed there as a reinforcement of the idea of an *intrinsic connection* between the human species and that of the plant kingdom. This ritual would encourage that connection to continue into the afterlife, knowing that the soul of the initiate-king would reincarnate in the future and again take up the unique responsibility with regard to food production here.

This connection was especially strong in those individual members of the population who were originally responsible for generating the impetus for the growth of vegetation during the creation period, many millions of years ago. These were the real kings (king = kin-g = kin of 'g' or geo, meaning earth) of the agricultural world and ultimately were responsible for feeding their people in later years. This is the real basis for an hereditary monarchy. Their genetic pattern would hopefully be reproduced through the blood line into future generations, thus protecting the harvest.

There are echoes of this knowledge in the sacrament known as Holy Communion in the Christian tradition. The statement *'This is my blood you drink, this is my body you eat'* – given in relationship to the wine and bread being shared – was an especially poignant expression of this esoteric knowledge. It would have been impossible to explain such a connection in any other understandable way at that time, without the science of genetics or biology. The timeless science of metaphysics had to be relied on again to illustrate this vital concept by the only means then possible. The mystical concepts of yesterday often find a new understanding in the sciences of today or tomorrow.

The human genetic code is like music. Each of us has our own frequency determined by our genetic makeup and, together, we produce the music of humanity, which blends with the music of this unique sphere, the planet Earth.

In many musical compositions there is a theme or phrase which recurs throughout the piece. Some human incarnations are destined to be part of this special central theme. Their energies bring humanity forward in a multi-dimensional melody of creation here on earth. Less obviously, the frequencies or vibrations of some people will produce the impetus for growth in the plant kingdom, so that we then produce enough food for the whole of the human population, providing we do not artificially manipulate the natural balance.

FENNEL

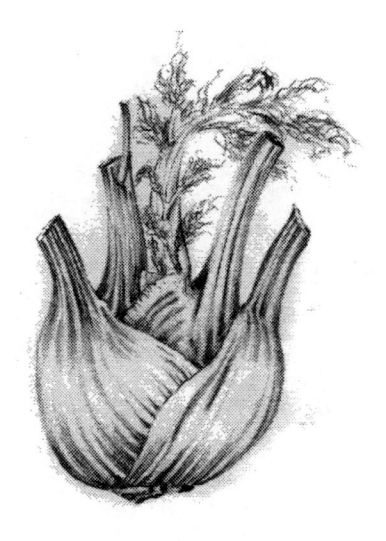

HUMAN HEART

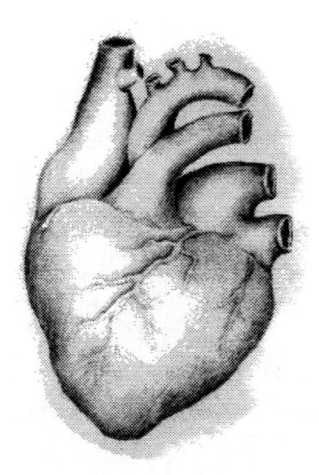

The impressions on these pages illustrate some of the reflections of our physical human presence into our environment. (There are other vegetables which reflect the inner chambers of the heart, such as tomato and capsicum.)

Tree

Human lung

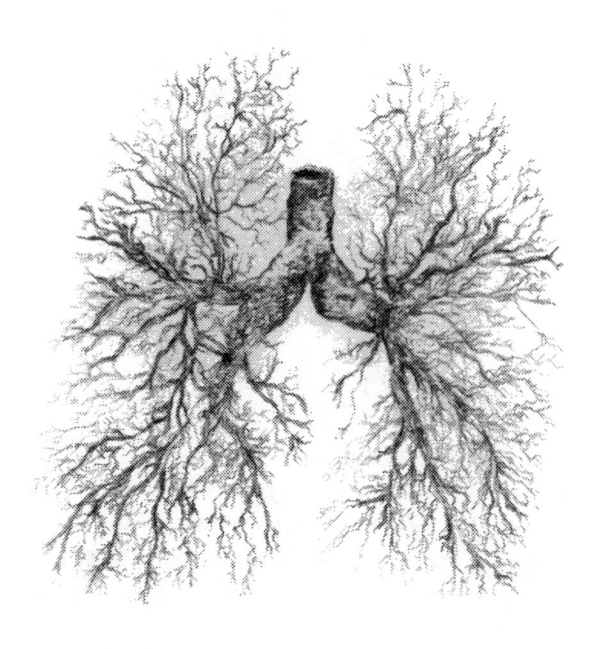

WALNUT (TOP & SIDE VIEW)

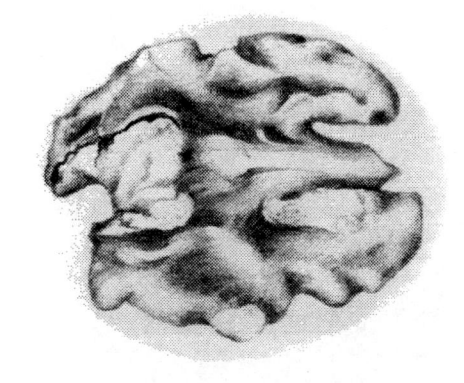

HUMAN BRAIN

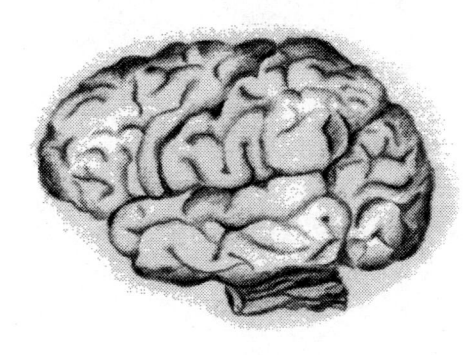

Carrot (cross section)

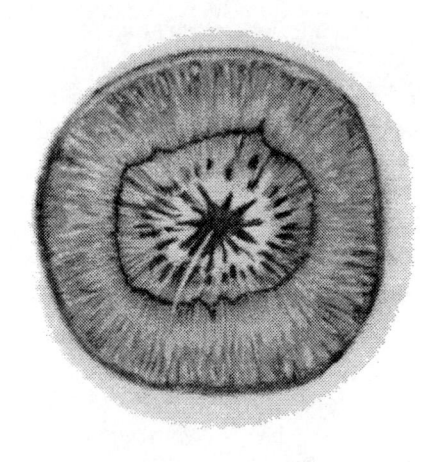

Human eye (pupil)

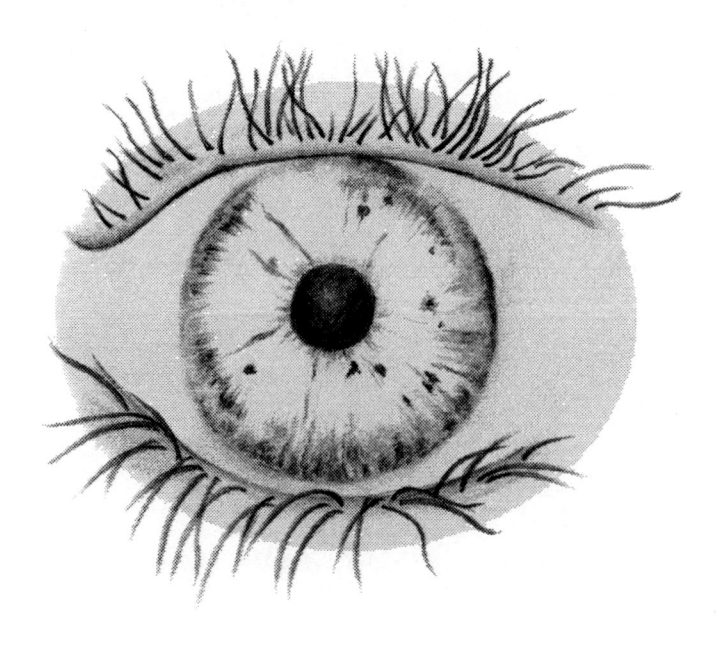

The inter-relatedness of the human evolutionary pattern and that of the plant kingdom is especially interesting. This connection has shown itself in other ways which we simply have failed to notice, partly because our present understanding of our own evolution is limited by Darwinian ideas.

The forests and trees help to maintain the exact balance of oxygen and carbon dioxide that we need to survive here, acting in some ways rather like the *lungs* of the planet. There is a hidden parallel between the way we have begun to destroy our own lungs by smoking cigarettes (people) and the destruction of the rain forests (planet). Given that our genetic blueprint was used in the creation of both the plant and animal kingdoms, the correlation is not really surprising.

The idea that *like cures like* is the basis of homoeopathic medicine. The idea is that there are mirrors of ourselves within plants and other substances and these can be used, in homoeopathic dilutions, to effect a cure for disease in humans. We have – in ourselves and our relationship to the whole planet – a delicately balanced interaction which we misunderstand at our peril. Some of these reflections are illustrated here. There are many more.

So, what happens when this mechanism begins to fail? Are there signposts along the way that we need to recognise if we are to avoid making inappropriate choices? There are some significant indicators which could imply the human>plant>food frequencies have been disrupted. They are:

– Human starvation. This should not occur in a balanced planetary organism.

– Stockpiling and wastage of produce. This confuses the planetary consciousness into misinterpreting the need and consequently it may begin to produce less or may adopt an irregular pattern of production.

- The correlation between genetic engineering in plants/seeds/grain and genetic engineering in humans. They are reflections of each other and are intrinsically linked together. Their progression will run in parallel.

- The correlation between the destruction of the forests and trees in the plant kingdom and our tendency to self-destruct human lung tissue by smoking cigarettes.

- Obesity in human beings. The imbalance reflects back on those in the human race who strive unconsciously to maintain the balance of human energies on the physical level. They will gain weight in direct opposition to those who starve and in direct proportion to their individual responsibility to maintain a planetary balance. They are unknowingly a balancing mechanism within humanity on a physical planetary level.

- Misuse and storage of other planetary energies, such as nuclear power. The connection here is with kundalini energy in humans, which when released slowly and progressively is a natural evolutionary event. When released suddenly or inappropriately, the effect can be devastating.

Human weight gain is also compounded by the rise in frequency level of the planet in response to the thinning of the ozone layer. More subtle energies are being absorbed directly by the human tissue and so progressively less food — and food of a different type — is now required. Unfortunately, the availability of almost every kind of food in western society, and the fact that this industry is a most powerful influence on our lives makes it almost impossible for us to recognise and adjust to these changes in a spontaneous and natural way.

If we had related to food differently, simply as a vital energy source rather than a social ritual, we would more quickly recognise that a change was occurring and adapt accordingly. As it is, our bodies now illustrate the problem for us and we need to learn to interpret the population weight increase in a different way. To try to regulate this imbalance by constant dieting and by unproductive exercise is bizarre, especially when other human beings starve. Some of the world's population barely have the physical energy reserves to walk, while we waste precious human energy pounding a treadmill in an attempt to redress a balance which we haven't yet begun to understand. In a way, those who carry extra weight also carry an aspect of the *conscience* of a global society.

The evolutionary development of the energy centres in the human subtle energy body is very different between people. Some individuals have already begun to open at the heart centre. This gradual opening enhances their intuitive abilities as well as giving a deeper level of personal and global conscience as these are attributes of the heart centre. Their personal connection to the planetary consciousness is closer and more acutely felt, and their personal responsibility increases in direct proportion to their evolutionary development especially where this energy centre is concerned. Once again, the word *heart* can be translated as *hear-t* which would be to *hear the earth* (hear + t as T is used here to symbolise the cross, the symbol of earth)

Often this increasing personal awareness is expressed as a deep concern for the environment and the welfare of people and animals. There is usually an effort to make personal choices which correspond to these views such as becoming vegetarian or vegan, recycling household waste and choosing natural fabrics for clothing. Natural fabrics allow energy to flow more easily and consistently within the subtle energy body and do not disturb the natural energy field in the same way as synthetics. This is especially important when choosing underwear such as bras, pants and underpants which are worn next to the skin. Man-made fibres are common in these articles of clothing and should be avoided. These choices are usually ecologically sound ones too, especially if we choose not to view animals as a source of food. Feeding grain to animals, which are then eaten by us, is a very inefficient way of utilising the energy resources available and the vegetarian choice is a practical one as well as often being healthier, and certainly less cruel. It also helps to raise our awareness on more subtle levels.

Subtle information is passed between individuals on a spiritual level with an intensity directly proportional to their evolutionary development or the closeness of their spiritual connection to each other. Therefore, subtle impressions and ideas will flow more easily between those to whom we are most closely linked by these subtle threads. These are members our *soul group*. Once again, we may be thousands of miles apart or may not have met at all in this particular incarnation. Time and distance are unimportant here, what is eternal and dynamic is the love-based spiritual threads which form these connections between us. *This is the real world-wide-web.*

The information that is transmitted can be on many levels – physical, emotional, mental and spiritual impressions and ideas can flow subconsciously between individuals. We may not realise where these impressions come from, or why we feel something strongly at a particular time. Often we will dismiss these ideas as daydreaming or something similar. However, what is happening to those who are close to us on this network is important, because if their well-being is seriously threatened we may pick up the echoes of the anxiety or fear without realising why. If those closest to us are starving, we may feel this hunger without realising that it is not our own, but belongs to those whose love-based energy threads still connect with our lives. This is especially tragic if it is one of our soul group whose life is plagued by poverty and hunger somewhere else in the world and we ignore those issues in our everyday life, feeling or pretending that they are not our concern.

Human energies need to be balanced on all levels.

Our own hunger may or may not be a physical need. It may be a manifestation of a spiritual or creative hunger if spiritual expression is missing from our lives for whatever reason. If someone close to us in our soul group has a similar missing component in their lives, then this can also be subtly transmitted to us, but may be translated differently by our own consciousness. We may just feel the sensation of physical need or craving, without realising the real spiritual nature of the impression or where it came from.

Our physical brain is an instrument which we use to access our personal consciousness or mind, which in turn is linked to a greater universal consciousness. The love-based threads join us together on the subtle human world-wide-web, itself reflected in the World Wide Web of our computers and the internet. Both stretch around the globe, across all cultures and nations.

This idea was one of many I was considering during my time in Finland because I especially enjoy thinking 'outside the box'.

Rovaniemi is a small town in Finnish Lapland, just inside the Arctic Circle. I studied there during the winter of 1996/7. One project was to write a short paper on *Shamanism and Healing in the North*. I was particularly interested in the beliefs of the indigenous peoples of North America and Australia and the opportunity to learn more about the indigenous people of Northern Europe – the Saami – was especially important to me. I remember gazing from my window over my keyboard across the snow and frozen pine trees around my apartment, while juggling with the piles of books and papers on my desk.

My home was close to the local school. Early each morning and every evening small groups of children would walk along the pathway to and from the school in their brightly coloured winter clothes. Some of the little boys wore bright red and blue hats with pointed ends, occasionally with little bells on each of the four points. These are called *The Four Winds* hats and are traditional headgear in Finnish Lapland, especially for children. The four individual points on the hats were originally meant to represent each of the points of the compass – the four winds. I thought of the parallel between the winds of the earth and the subtle energy flows within the human energy body, something known at the *karmic winds* in Tibetan medicine, and I made a mental note to follow up this idea later, as my studies included complementary medicine.

The connection between the Finnish people and the natural elements is unsurprising as Lapland has always been known as *the place where winds are born*. The belief that some Finnish people are born with a natural ability to affect the winds is a very old one and was one of the reasons why Finnish sailors were not popular members of the crews of sailing ships. However, Finnish witches and wizards were traditionally sought by sailors with the conviction that winds could be bought from them to benefit their voyages.

This is a harsh northern climate with winter temperatures of around minus 30°C and lower, with bitter winds driving snowstorms across the Arctic Circle. I walked and rode my bike through some of those snows that winter. It must have been quite a strange sight as I pedalled away on my tricycle through the snow to the library and the university. During this time I learned a little more about the snow itself and how the Inuit and the Saami peoples have so many words to describe it. There are over three hundred words for the different types of snow in these languages, each word defining something special about a particular snowfall or an aspect of the snow which is unique. This information is absolutely essential to people living and herding reindeer through this arctic landscape.

The snowflakes themselves are individually unique, each constructed in a completely different pattern to any other snowflake. Snow becomes an exciting world in itself when it is viewed as millions of individual snowflakes, each having a unique identity, each an original form in itself.

It is similar to the way in which each of us, as human beings are unique, and at least some of that uniqueness depends on *the human bar-code*.

SNOWFLAKE

Every snowflake is individual and this is an impression of just one snowflake in many millions of different patterns. Perhaps what we are looking at when we see the magnification of each snowflake is, essentially, a type of memory pattern in the frozen water.

Looking at snow as a huge collection of individual unique flakes is fascinating. There are some insights – from the study of homoeopathy in particular – which make it even more relevant. The idea that forms the basis for homoeopathic medicine – *that water holds a memory* – is one such insight.

Perhaps what we are looking at when we see the magnification of each snowflake is, essentially, *a type of memory pattern* in the frozen water.

Is it possible that the special way in which water retains its memory of a substance, even after dilution has washed away all physical traces of it (as in the preparation of the homoeopathic remedies) can be glimpsed on a planetary level in the millions of unique patterns in the snowflakes? Is this coded water-memory a secret store of information contained in all of the water on this planet? This pattern may not only relate to physical substances whose memory is retained in the memory pattern of the water. Perhaps many different kinds of information can be held there including the memory of *emotional* energy patterns. Everything, in fact, that has ever happened here within this enclosed environment of our planet Earth.

The memory patterns are already there in the water when it falls as rain, but only when this water is solidified as snowflakes does it begin to reveal its potentially stunning secret.

In the planetary water cycle, less than 5% of the water is fresh. The remainder is salt or sea water. Most of our fresh water is locked away in the ice caps. The sun evaporates water from the oceans and rivers and this falls to earth as rain or snow later. The indigenous peoples of the arctic regions have long held the view that there are 'people' locked in the ice and have treated the ice cliffs and plateaux with reverence, in much the same way as other ethnic groups treat the burial places and sacred sites of their ancestors.

Could it be that what is buried in the ice is *the planetary memory* of the people who lived here before us, encapsulated in the patterns of the frozen water? The connection between water and energy lines – ley lines – is well documented. This energy network is part of the original creative energy matrix.

The water which passes through our bodies takes on our physical, emotional and mental energies and then transports them back into the environment. It permeates the earth and rocks, producing in some places a hard copy recording of our lives and all of the events on planet Earth for millions of years (many instances of apparitions and other phenomena are found in close proximity to sandstone rocks which are known to be very porous).

The winds carry the water, as rains or snow, across our land masses where it eventually falls as rain in areas where our staple foods, such as corn and wheat, are grown. It is essential for plant growth.

Encapsulated in that water, is the vital information regarding our genetic makeup and life patterns, which forms the link between our genetic code and plant growth world-wide. *The two elements are linked, and the means of making this connection is in the water — with its memory — which is carried on the wind.*

The grain harvest is dependent on much more than the weather. It is also linked to the population of human beings in incarnation at any one time, and this information may also be available through the energy patterns in the water. The harvest produced should be proportionate to the number of people we need to feed. The fact that many millions of people either starve or live just above starvation level may be a result of our insistence on division and separation within the human population, and on the fact that we have somehow detached ourselves from our agricultural roots and now treat the harvest as a commodity rather than a living process.

This behaviour produces, in ourselves, an attempt to balance the equation by allowing — as a result of their genetic variation or programming — some human beings to carry excess weight to compensate for those in the population world-wide who are starving. The growing problem of obesity within the western world will not be easily resolved, but we could begin by doing more to share the stores of produce we hold in Europe and America with those who are under-fed in the rest of the world. This would be just the first step in redressing the balance. Our urgent need is to view the planet as a whole. The amount of food produced is in direct proportion to the population — but on a world-wide basis. Any variation will produce an imbalance both in the harvest (the planet) and in the way we store this surplus energy in our bodies (the people).

The spiritual means of connection between individuals worldwide is via the subtle energy lines – and the earth grid. We exchange information – and energy – via this network. Subconsciously, we are aware of those others who connect directly to ourselves on this network and we will unknowingly receive and transmit some subtle information between each other. This information will include anything which adds to the evolutionary process of mankind and also anything which threatens our existence, including starvation. The subtle message passed along these energy lines will convey hunger and trigger in some people the subconscious need to correct that balance – to eat – even though in our own environment there is no such threat. We are connected world-wide to each other and the subconscious trigger to eat more, even when we are experiencing excessive weight gain, is because on some level we have acknowledged this connection and are attempting to redress the world-human-energy balance.

To recap: the human genetic code has a similar function to the bar-codes we find in our supermarkets and other retail establishments. It identifies us as the individuals we are and forms the blueprint for our human makeup. Just as the bar-code in the supermarket signals when stocks of one particular type of product are running low, so our genetic code signals when an individual who is part of the planet's creative and evolutionary process is about to leave physical incarnation.

In this way, the human circles of individuals who are essential to the creative process on this planet are maintained constantly. Those who are committed to maintaining the evolutionary process on this planet return here regularly to carry on in this assignment.

It is an act of love.

Human energy is stored as fat in our tissues and, because we are connected to each other across huge planetary distances, we can receive subtle subconscious signals which alert us to the fact that someone close to us on this network is experiencing some kind of deprivation. *This can be a spiritual need just as much as a physical one.* This impetus will often produce the need to eat more than we need and so to store extra energy in an attempt to redress the balance.

The network is one for transmission of information and subtle energies and has been with us since the beginning of the creation process here on Earth. *It is the way in which many great ideas were transmitted over different continents and took root at the same time in various cultures and locations.*

Water and wind are predominantly the practical means by which the information is recorded and carried within the planetary whole. The past is accurately recorded in the water and the future is, in effect, carried by the wind.

CHAPTER SIX

The Virgin Stones

Stonehenge is perhaps the best known of the stone circles in the British Isles although there are many other impressive circles including those at Arbor Low, Castlerigg and in the Orkneys.

There has been speculation about their possible function as an astronomical or astrological observatory, an ancient temple or place of worship, or a strategic energy point in the ley network. It is likely that the stone circles were all of these things.

In the right framework, and in a knowledgeable society, none of those possibilities would be incompatible with any of the others. The stone circles would have been a focal point for all of these activities in a society which accepted the study of the stars and the universe as a sacred science and used that knowledge to structure its survival and well-being.

When we take a close look at our significant places of worship today, such as the cathedrals and churches, we find that most are built around a set of ideas which are encapsulated in the actual stones of the building. The structure of most church buildings reflects the symbol of the cross itself and so the main theme or image of that particular belief system – Christianity – is actually built into the stones of the building.

When the remains of these churches are discovered in many thousands of years time, another society or civilisation may wonder about the significance of the shape of the cross in the arrangement of the stones. The images and ideas relating to the belief system which the building protects and mirrors might be lost, but we can begin to guess at the purpose of the original building by the arrangement of the stones and remaining foundations.

The stone circles are the same. **They embody an idea within their fabric.**

Their function as an astronomical observatory was only part of their real purpose, which was to illustrate a sacred concept and to preserve this information forever within the positioning and fabric of the stones themselves.

They were built to last for thousands of years because this knowledge was so very precious to mankind for the future, because the idea they illustrated was also part of the human initiatory process and information the stone circles held has remained a secret to those outside the circle of human initiates on this planet.

These are those among us whose purpose it is to safeguard and protect the ancient sacred knowledge. Their unwritten – and often unconscious – code is one based on universal truth and unconditional love.

These are known as the *virgins* or *pure* who reincarnate within each generation, and in every country of the world to ensure that the original transmission or blueprint for the evolution of humanity on this planet, which is encoded into their being, is always present.

They are connected to each other in a particular sequence on a highly spiritual level and together they form part of a select soul group. Sometimes they work absolutely alone, especially when their particular energies are needed for a unique part of the evolutionary process. Even in this isolation, they still maintain their spiritual link with the circle.

At times they connect in a practical way with a soul mate or twin/primary soul. This is especially necessary in some areas of work where trust and sharing of responsibility come into play. Sometimes this is a triad or triangular configuration ... *which is reflected in the arrangement of the stones in Stonehenge.*

The three-connection of one vertical pillar with two horizontal stones is the pattern which links the initiatory circle throughout the planet. This triad arrangement of stones cannot stand without linking into a circular configuration, although its neighbouring triad of two uprights and one vertical stone can stand alone as the central giant stones do. Stonehenge was created in direct correspondence with the planetary web. This web contains the energy centres which are held and maintained by a linked-hierarchy of initiates and adepts throughout the planet.

Sometimes the initiate is fully aware of the purpose of their work in a particular incarnation, but most often they will continue throughout their lives without this conscious knowledge. On a higher spiritual level they will be following the universal plan which was embedded into their consciousness many millions of years ago, at the beginning of creation.

They communicate subconsciously with each other, most often without realising that they belong to this network or in any way acknowledging that it exists. Their work and ideas will evolve spontaneously in different parts of the world within the same time period. This partly explains why, even as far back as the time when the pyramids were built, people in different countries speaking different languages and having no other means of communicating over long distances would work on a particular project, invention, building programme or other evolutionary idea *at the same time*. They are linked by the web or network of subtle energy or light lines which link all of the light-workers on this planet, whether or not they are aware of their spiritual connection to each other. The initiates form the main energy points on this network. *They are the spiritual Stonehenge – the virgin stones.* Their position here is vital to the whole web and only those capable of withstanding the enormous, but often subconscious, pressure of this special place can take up their point, position, or node on this hidden web.

Stonehenge represents this circle of initiates. The stones both represent those who are linked on this network and also illustrate how they are linked together. Stonehenge also illustrates the part of the initiation process which finally allows access to this sacred circle. The stones are there for the initiates of each generation to see and recognise, if only on a subconscious level.

For those rare individuals going through the final initiation process within this lifetime, the stones remain so that they may see the significance of what has happened to them.

The final initiation process is, by its intense nature, a devastatingly painful and lonely experience. The pressures to be withstood by the candidate for initiation before he or she can take their place in the circle of initiates are extreme.

The life of the Master Jesus was also an illustration and example of the final initiation experience. Because the *New Testament* is written on at least three different levels of understanding, this initiatory pattern is well hidden. The information remains unavailable to those who have not raised their own spiritual awareness or have not yet shared in this particular experience.

The standing stones remain as an epitaph to a process of human evolutionary experience which still continues today. They are there to be recognised and understood by those for whom their purpose is most important and relevant. They remain a mystery to others, even when the idea is explained to them, because each of us can only bring our personal experience to this hypothesis. The initiatory process is essentially an *internalised* experience which takes place in the life of the individual, but which may be entirely unrecognised even by those closest to that person.

The ancient purpose of the initiation process was to test each candidate to ensure that they were ready and suitably prepared for the intense pressure to which they were about to be exposed within the circle itself.

Originally, sound and vibration were the tools of creation and also the means of transmission from one energy centre to another. These were the high frequency energies for which the initiates within the circle were prepared. This flow of vibrational energy followed the lines of light, which were the original ley lines. The foundation or blue-print for the creative process was relayed and transmitted globally in this way.

Only those who were capable of withstanding, holding and then transmitting these energies could naturally take their place within the circle. The trials of the individual are equal to the level of responsibility of the position. Innate wisdom, quiet personal strength and the capacity to love unconditionally are just some of the vital ingredients within the circle. The process of initiation involves the development and opening of energy centres within the subtle energy-body. There is a particular pattern to this development process which is illustrated here.

In initiates this flow of energy – known as kundalini – is forced or quickened. The experience of those going through this process is unique and entirely different from that of humanity as a whole. In most of us the gradual opening of the centres is not a conscious event but a natural part of evolution, taking place over many millions of years. It cannot compare to the traumatic and often agonising experience of those in whom this development is speeded up. They are effectively compressing the slow, gradual evolutionary experience into the space of a few short lifetimes.

This process results in a period of great mental, emotional and spiritual turmoil in which the individual must confront everything of concern in their own nature – past and present – before they are able to move on. It may be a long period of intensive self-

STONEHENGE

A familiar view of Stonehenge, Wiltshire at dawn. This impression illustrates the position of the heel-stone in relationship to the sunrise at the summer solstice, viewed from within the circle.

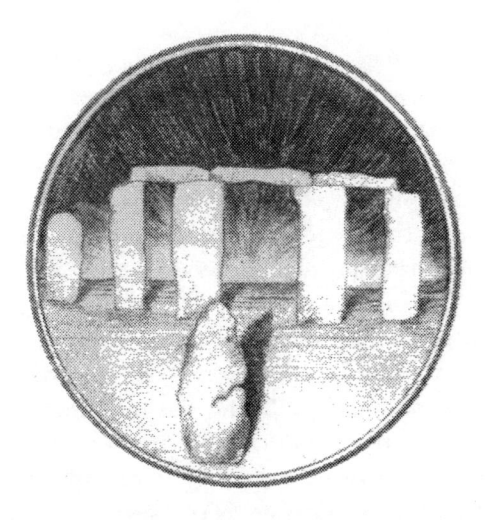

An impression of the view from behind the heel-stone at dawn on the summer solstice. The shadow from the heel-stone penetrates the circle.

appraisal, coloured by the full awakening of our *internal conscience and intuition* within the energy centre of the heart.

Every fear is magnified and must be confronted and worked through. Emotional pain has to be released and healed, and all physical attachments need to be eventually relinquished. This is a time of great personal and spiritual growth but also a time of trial and unseen agony, and one of complete aloneness.

The individual needs also to learn how to deal with their own raised levels of sensitivity because they are now super-sensitive to other people's energies on every level.

Until this point in their lives, they can usually interact relatively easily within the society in which they live. Sometimes this relationship is strained, but it is still possible to live within society in an accepted way, even if considered to be slightly out of step or eccentric. This is partly because the values of the individual may no longer be reflected in their immediate environment and their choices, based on those changed values, will be different from those of the majority.

Eventually, living continuously within society becomes progressively more difficult. The experiences gained in the initiatory experience need to be consolidated within the character of the individual, and this progression takes time. The increased sensitivity, often accompanied by gifts of deeper intuition or clairvoyance, make the individual extremely vulnerable during this transition time.

For some people this period of adjustment is one of just a few years, but it can be that the process is experienced throughout the lifetime of the adept. During this time they may find it impossible to cope with the expectations of everyday life, because they are changed and their personal experience has set them apart from everyone they once knew.

It is part of a transition process.

The individual needs to learn to stand alone and to depend entirely on their own intuition and judgement. It is an essential process, because their own choices and ideas will eventually influence many others. This may not be in this particular lifetime but in another incarnation in the future.

No amount of time could ever adequately prepare us for this deeply personal evolutionary experience. Because of its nature, the experience usually arrives unexpectedly. If the individual were more aware of what was to come then the full impact of the experience would be lost. This is a time of intense challenge, change and spiritual growth and the circumstances for this initiatory event will only present themselves at a point when the individual is ready to receive and to survive them.

Before the energy-centres within the head can begin to unfold, there are some very real challenges to be confronted. Individual personal development and courage must be sufficient to withstand the incredible pressure and pain resulting from compressing the rising fiery energies – kundalini – into the skull cavity. This is an experience comparable to pumping white-hot volcanic lava continually into a sealed fine china vessel.

These fiery energies cannot reside for long within the relatively small space of the human skull. After opening the energy centre at the brow, known as the *ajna* centre, the fiery stream flows onwards towards the centre at the top of the head known as the *crown* centre or *sahasrara*.

The flow of (kundalini) energy begins to burn its way through to the top of the head. It eventually produces a cascade of brilliant light – for those with vision tuned to see it – and a fountain of flowing energy from the crown chakra. This is a *halo*, now surrounding the head.

The circle of fire experienced around the top of the head as the kundalini energy finds its way towards the crown centre is excruciatingly painful. It feels like hundreds of tiny white-hot rmed together in a tight band around the head. This is internal experience of the *crown of thorns* described in terms in the Christian gospels.

The stinging stabs of pain form a circle around the skull, which would resemble the pain caused by a woven crown of hawthorn or some similar thorny shrub, formed into a circular crown and pressed tightly on to the head. The difference is that the real thorns from the hawthorn shrub would be an *external* experience and what is experienced here with the raising of kundalini energy is an entirely *internal* event. It is almost impossible to compare the two experiences in this way, but the idea of a crown of thorns is about as close as we can get to the internal event when we try to express it as a physical reality.

Before the intensely hot flow of energy can reach the energy centres in the head, it must be transmuted by an energy centre at the base of the skull, known as Alta Major centre or Alta Major chakra.

Alta Major centre acts as a transformer, it becomes a holding station for the rising fiery flow of energy.

Kundalini energy is the human equivalent of atomic power, and this is the *baptism of fire* described by the apostles and some of the saints. The resulting changes in the flow of energy through the human energy-body produces a brilliant explosion of light around the head – the halo effect.

The crystal skulls which have been found in some parts of the world may well have been created to try to illustrate this phenomena or process. The white hot molten glass filling the mould, then producing a clear, almost transparent, crystal skull would have been one way of demonstrating something of this hidden experience.

The creation process was one of sound and vibration. Each of the individuals in the circle would bring their own particular tone or vibration. This unique personal note of the individual is expressed fully for the first time at the moment the fiery kundalini energy enters the skull cavity. It is then unconsciously sounded and recognised amongst fellow initiates in the future.

Those at the centre of the circle have the higher frequency sound within their own individual energy field and would probably be most capable of withstanding the transmission of very high frequency energies. These fiery energies were part of the creation process and their echoes are still here in the English language.

When 'S' appears at the beginning of a word it can give the impression of wind or fire. The shushing sound of the letter S is so reminiscent of the shoosh of flame or the softer sound of rushing air, rather like a strong wind. In the the word stone, the resemblance to the word tone, as in music, becomes obvious. The S in the word stone is significant. It indicates heat or fire or the connection with hissing air. The word stone then becomes *s-tone* which, very roughly interpreted, means a fire or windsound. The picture grows into one of wind, intense heat or fire and the resulting sound or tone produced.

Each *stone* or initiate within the circle would be capable of withstanding the elemental energies which produced the vibrational sound of creation. (They would themselves be a circle of *s-tones*.)

The stone circles or henges remain to testify to the constant presence of that circle of initiates within each generation and every society. They are a representation in stone of something which is very much alive among us today in all walks of life, from politics, religion, art, music and commerce – a group of people who are connected (whether they are aware of it or not) to each other, with the sole purpose of implementing the original plan for the creation and evolution of this planet.

They may not hold the same views, support the same political parties or any political ideal. They may be of one particular religion, or none at all. Some are gifted in a particular way, perhaps in art, theatre or music while others sit quietly in the background in a supporting role. Some would be considered very ordinary characters and unremarkable in the way they live their lives. They pass unnoticed in our communities and would probably be the first to admit that they do not consider their lives to be especially significant in any noticeable way. Others are very famous people.

If we questioned any of these individuals more closely we would probably find that their hope is for world peace and understanding between people and their efforts within their own personal sphere are geared towards making the world a better place to live in. If we questioned their friends, we would invariably find that they felt the world was a better place for their presence, and their presence is always there, in each generation, for millions of years.

Sometimes these individuals are drawn towards particular energy lines and may take up residence in these significant places. These particular places may not appear in any way extraordinary and could be absolutely anywhere on the planet from our towns and cities to the countryside and mountains. *It is only when we view the landscape from a subtle energy perspective that these points may suddenly appear dynamic.*

These were the original transmission lines used during the creation process and are still active in transmitting energies for the evolution of the planet. An individual whose life is apparently very ordinary may, in fact, be holding a position on one of the energy lines which is vital to the transmission of evolutionary ideas and information. He or she may have been drawn to that position by the particular vibration or frequency level of the place or may find that circumstances conspire to make their living in that particular location essential.

Our freedom to choose where we live is not always such a personal decision as we may imagine, and what we sometimes consider to be rather ordinary, insignificant lives may, in fact, be a crucial link in the great creative process which is going on all around us here on this planet.

Our own personal vibratory note – which is the complete total energy of all our entire being, including our genetic component – is an essential part of the present creative process here on Earth. The place where we live and the people we meet form the location of our note in the song. There are some places where the presence of a particular individual is crucial to the composition and, in turn, they will feel especially drawn to that particular place. Even if they are not eventually content or happy in that location, it may prove impossible to leave. The fates usually conspire to keep these individuals where they are most needed, while their freedom of choice always appears – to the world and very often to themselves – to remain intact.

Some of us sense all of this already, at a deep level within our consciousness. Every time we break a thread between one another we feel a sense of loss. When we do this in anger, by our arguments, fights and ultimately wars, we threaten our own life-support network.

The threads that link us to each other are life-giving. It is a world-wide web of people linked by subtle energies flowing along interconnected lines. We literally have no idea who might be the next connection to ourselves on the universal web. It could be anyone, someone in another country, another culture with a different political agenda or a completely different religion. Our transient commitment to peace and universal brotherhood is suddenly transformed into our own personal survival mechanism, because if we do not make this our aim then we risk our own self-destruction.

The person whose needless death we ignore in another country may well be the next person along our own thread of life.

This is also the secret of the muse.

Often, a musician, artist or writer will draw on some invisible source of inspiration. The feeling of linking in to an energy source of great creativity is often described as working with a muse or some other inspirational being. This muse can be a *real person* who is linked to the creative artist by the subtle energy links we have described. Often the ideas for songs, paintings and stories are *channelled* from some other source on the energy web. This is invariably another individual who is close to us in frequency level within our soul group but who may be living an apparently normal life within society, but one where collective life experience (past lives and present) makes it possible to transmit the ideas needed for the work. It is her soul-song.

The secret of the muse is not easily uncovered as her (the role of the muse is traditionally female, although there is no reason why this cannot be a masculine role) transmissions to the composer or artist are entirely subconscious, although she may sometimes recognise the result of her inspirational influence in their work, and wonder.

There is also the possibility that the muse may not be in physical incarnation. However, it is easier and safer when a particular work of significance is required for her to be on the physical plane at the same time as the creative artist. Distance, culture, colour, wealth, everything in fact in their lives may be different, but the line of communication which has always been available between them still exists. It remains because it is love-based and the energies of universal love were the original energies of creation. These lines can never be destroyed.

We have abused the word *love* in recent years, and this casual usage has truly undermined the real meaning of the word. The next level of existence beyond our physical level here on Earth is one of pure love. Somehow we have blurred the true spiritual concept of real love, so that when we say that there is a level of consciousness which is one of pure spiritual love, it is almost impossible for us to understand this idea.

The love that exists on that level is unconditional love. It is universal and its energy already permeates every atom of our being, but we are presently almost entirely unconscious of its existence. This is the real – spiritual – meaning of being in love.

The energies encountered here are all-encompassing and completely non-judgemental in character. The feelings we have when we say we are in love today are only the faintest reflection of this deep extraordinary pure love existing on that higher frequency.

On one level, this feels just like being wrapped in a soft, warm blanket and gently held, safe and deeply cared for and fully understood. There is total acceptance in this love energy of everything we are or have ever been. There is a magnificent expansion of spiritual understanding. All knowledge is there and it is available to us directly in proportion to our capacity to embrace and hold it.

The full experience of this level of consciousness can only be compared to the ecstasy of the most excruciatingly rich and intense orgasm, but where our physical orgasm explodes and fades, this endures and does not immediately fade away.

Our physical brain is the instrument which we use to access this level of consciousness but our ability to assimilate is related to how far our own spiritual understanding has developed. The human initiation process severely tests the individual in this way and the assimilation of the knowledge gained in the initiation experience itself can be a long one. Sometimes it takes many years and much depends on the depth of knowledge transmitted and the capacity for this understanding in the individual.

The spiritually orgiastic nature of this experience raises the initiate to a higher level of consciousness and fuses their consciousness with that higher plane. The result is an ability – from this point onwards – to re-connect with these love energies almost at will.

The sheer magnificence of this total experience is beyond words. These are the energies of the original creation process. They are also the energies which forged the spiritual links between the *virgins* or *pure* ones involved in the creation process here on Earth. This love-based energy is all that is needed to hold them and link them to each other in every incarnation, because their need and purpose is to return here over many millions of years in order to further the evolution of this planet.

The individuals concerned are usually totally unaware of these connections and their experience is often undetectable from the life experience of any other evolved human being. Sometimes these evolved souls meet along the pathways of life and they will experience, somewhere deep in their hearts, the stirring of recognition of one of their companions. They could be working in completely different fields, perhaps separated by thousands of miles, but the feeling of having met before or of some kind of recognition or attraction between them will come when contact is made.

What they have in common is the unspoken commitment to humanity and the need to contribute in some way towards its future. This contribution may simply be made just by being here, incarnate at this particular time. Our unique individual subtle energy field may be all that is needed from us to further the evolutionary process here on Earth, especially if this individual is placed in a location which links that person's subtle energies most strongly into the planetary grid at that exact point.

Sometimes the energies in that particular location need raising or stabilising in some way. We may never know what we contribute or why we live in one particular place, but the consequences of our being there can have far reaching effects on the planetary whole, far beyond our imagination. The subtle energy lines of connection between ourselves and the members of our original creative group still remain. There is an unconscious communication between each member of the group which collectively strives to ensure that they remain in harmony, even though their individual lives may be very different from each other.

When one of them dies that connection still remains.

A balance has to be maintained between those who are incarnate and those who are not at any one time. If the balance swings so that more individuals in one part of the connective web have died and moved on from physical incarnation then things must change. The lives of those individuals who remain incarnate will come to a close as they prepare to move on with their group. Their position has become untenable on a physical level.

Once this is clearly understood, it becomes impossible to kill, injure or in any way hurt another human being, because (apart from any other consideration) in doing so we may endanger our own existence. If we fail to recognise the individuals who are connected to us on the subtle – but direct – web of existence, then we risk injuring ourselves by hurting them.

It is vital information and must be worth repeating.

Until now, we have not had the means to destroy whole segments of the planetary web in one action. Nuclear power can do this, as the events of Hiroshima and Nagasaki proved. The planetary web was broken at that time and a large area of the subtle energy body of the planet was completely destroyed at an atomic level. The present hole in the protective ozone layer surrounding our planet may well be a direct consequence of these particular actions, and this may not be the only consequence.

Atomic power destroys on many levels and we have not yet understood the hidden effect of its use against people. The next century will, I hope, show more of the real meaning of love, if only because we have no way of knowing what all our connections to others are on the energy web, but that they are all vital to our own survival here will eventually become apparent when our information technology reaches maturity.

When enough of the links are severed on this physical level then our own life energy here becomes isolated and our physical incarnation is no longer supported.

Both male and female initiates are linked together by unconditional love, regardless of their sex or sexuality. Their particular sexual orientation may well reflect their own place in the circle and their relationships with others may not necessarily be celibate, although sometimes this is essential. Heterosexual, bi-sexual and homosexual partnerships have all produced exactly the right energies for an individual to function in the work they must complete. The focus on sexuality is essentially one based in this particular time period on this planet, and the real love-based links are what is important, whether or not the relationship has a sexual element. Sometimes sex can be a wonderful way of expressing this deep spiritual connection between individuals, and it can also seal the physical bond between them, leaving them free to work in the world together. There are other equally deeply committed relationships between these individuals which do not include a physical sexual relationship. Both are fine and equally valid. Both rely on the deep spiritual love which is eternal, and all are reflected in the idea of the arrangement of the stones.

Some of the stone circles were built to be incredibly accurate astronomical observatories. There are obvious advantages in knowing the astronomical signposts in a society dependant on agriculture, hunting and fishing.

At Stonehenge, a second highly spiritual purpose is illustrated. At the summer solstice the initiation process described earlier can be shown – the summer solstice being a significant time when the sun was guaranteed to rise at a particular point above one special stone. The brilliance and heat of the sun would then illustrate the true nature of that human process.

Research has shown that at Stonehenge the stones with higher frequency vibratory levels are concentrated at the centre of circle and those with lower frequencies are on the outside. The stones in the centre give a completely different set of frequency readings when exposed to a series of sounds on the same frequency level.

There could well be a correlation between this and the different levels of initiation required to work within the human circle. The stones of the henge, when viewed *musically* or as pure *sound* energies could be compared to a grand orchestra (ore-chest-ra = mineral/stone-air/wind/breath/-sun) and it is no coincidence that the usual grouping of musicians in a conventional orchestra places the instruments with the highest sounds in the central positions. The conductor stands at the front, in a central position also. This position compares to the heel stone and it is the place of the individual who must *conduct* those fiery energies – represented by the rising sun – during the final part of the initiation process.

The original creative energies flowed between the individuals in a triangular pattern illustrated by Stonehenge and those energies still flow today, both on spiritual, emotional and, sometimes, on physical levels.

The mechanism is still one of light, sound and vibration but the way in which those original energies were combined and flowed has been partly concretised into our dense physical level of existence.

This lower, coarser frequency also now produces our present monetary system, which is, in fact, another network of creative energy. Its origins were in the exchange of more subtle energies and information between each of the individuals who were part of the original creative process here. Money has become a way for us to exchange energy between each other on this lower, dense, physical level in a very practical and material way.

Sound on this level is changed too and our speech patterns are now only a crude reflection of the higher, spiritually creative sounds, leaving only vestiges of these sacred sounds in our everyday language.

The individuals who reincarnate again and again to maintain the evolutionary structure within this planet were sometimes known as *virgins*. The word is used here to mean pure and it does not always follow that these individuals remain celibate for the whole of their many incarnations, although this is possible.

However, it does mean that their karmic record (this is the total record of all of their actions in each incarnation) is reconciled swiftly, usually within each lifetime. These individuals are able to recognise, if they wish to do so, the cause and effect of all of their actions in ways which most human beings would find impossible. This also means that they are born without sin which is another way of saying that they bring a clear karmic record into each of their incarnations. They are, therefore, free to take on board inherited family karmic issues needing resolution or to devote their lives to a particular work for humanity, unencumbered by personal issues left unresolved from past lives. Some will choose to carry a large part of the karmic inheritance of the group in any one incarnation, leaving others free to work without this restriction. Others are prepared to make the greater sacrifice of carrying some of the karmic inheritance of humanity as a whole.

The virgins rarely know who they really are, but it could be that they intuitively feel themselves to be different in some way from other people, probably rationalising their differences with far less esoteric explanations. This may be a necessary part of their evolutionary process. In order to do their work they need to fit in alongside everyone else in society, going their way mostly unnoticed and seldom recognised as being in any way different or standing out from the crowd, unless their work requires them to take a leading role in the society in which they live.

This may be in an area where their contribution will count most towards the progress of humanity and this contribution happens in many ways. There are people in all walks of life, including the film and music industries, whose presence is directly connected to the web of initiates and whose work is towards the greater good of humanity where the impetus is part of the planetary evolutionary process. *Virgins* are connected by the original love-based subtle threads but they otherwise live very different lives. This may sometimes mean that they appear at odds with each other over politics, religion or other cultural issues. The energies that bind them together are love energies on highly spiritual frequencies, so that even when these individuals find themselves in disagreement with each other in their physical lives, it is usually possible to bridge those differences eventually. The politics of world peace and the possibility of understanding between the world religions will depend to a large extent on the work of these individuals.

Whenever there is a problem with this spiritual connection between world initiates, it is most usually one of *failure to love*. It can occur when for some reason the heart centre of an individual is not connecting fully with those who are seeking to sustain that subtle connection on the higher levels. There can be many reasons why this can happen, but when it does, it causes a breach in the web of subtle energies and does not allow for the vital flow of creative energies within the circle of individuals. This then disrupts the energy flow, eventually causing some individuals to carry more of the load and so to sustain greater stress, and effectively isolating others. It also can, in the worst scenario, cause a complete break of the linkage of the circle for a short time thus allowing the protective energies towards humanity and the planet to be severely depleted.

The living circles, when complete and fully sustained, form a protective barrier within humanity itself which helps to counterbalance the karmic influences which are inherent in a population which has not yet realised its true identity.

Breaks in the circle are rarely a deliberate or conscious act by those concerned, rather a failure to recognise their real purpose here and that of others to whom they connect via those subtle spiritual links.

We are not born with our true identities and a life-road-map tucked under our arm. It takes time to realise who we really are.

CHAPTER SEVEN

A Reflection of Another Dimension

Everything we are is an exact reflection, in physical matter, of an already existing spiritual state. There have been times in our past when we were much closer to this other parallel existence, when we could more clearly perceive its qualities and reality. At that time the link between the spiritual and physical world was much stronger.

There are still places on our planet where the energies of this higher, more subtle plane can be felt. These are the sacred places found in every country and culture, many of which have been claimed by our great religions for themselves and become the sites for their churches and temples.

Some people can more easily shift their own consciousness to connect to this higher spiritual level. The practice of meditation will often begin to align our consciousness with that deeper, more profound awareness that regular, quiet, contemplation reveals. There are those who are born with this awareness already very strong and continually functioning throughout their lives. In some cultures these people were chosen as the shaman, priests, healers or other spiritual leaders of the community.

Another expression of this spiritual aspect is in mediumship, channelling and some healing methods such as Spiritual

Healing, Reiki and Therapeutic Touch. The field of alternative or complementary medicine has given a necessary focus for expression of these skills in our western society by some of those who feel this spiritual connection in some way.

Spirituality is often experienced as something outside our everyday lives, something different and sometimes rather exclusive. There is another perspective.

What if the ordinary, everyday reality in which we find ourselves was the very key to experiencing something altogether different, something almost magical? Suppose everything we do, say, build, invent or create is really an expression in physical terms of another — already existing — higher dimension? A dimension which we can begin to glimpse when we start to open our own consciousness to our spiritual nature and the reality of our true position in the universe.

To do this it helps if we can make the switch from believing that we are entirely the result of the Darwinian evolutionary process to knowing that our spiritual selves were part of the original creation process. Once we make that change in our perception, some other interesting ideas can begin to flow. It is rather like moving to another location to get a better view.

For example — in western countries, the two most common major purchases in our lives at the beginning of the twenty-first century would probably be our house and our car.

Allowing for the huge differences of culture, climate and wealth in the world — which are considerations affecting all our choices — then our house can come to *represent* our spiritual house or our true home on a higher level of consciousness. When we listen to the word itself carefully, we can almost hear something else. House becomes *how-see* or *how-we-see* ourselves? The fragile clues to these higher, spiritual pictures are there, hidden in our language already.

This idea is echoed in the Chinese art of feng shui (feng shui = wind and water) or geomancy. This is a technique which tries to reflect into our surroundings the harmonious aspects of a more spiritual existence. The way we arrange our house, our choice of colour (this often can indicate our soul or personality rays or vibrational frequency) and the things we value within our living space are all expressions of something much greater.

The idea, in feng shui, of creating a harmonious balance of energies within our home environment with a good strong flow of *chi* or *prana* (the subtle universal energy) throughout our home is such a good one. The old idea of *as above so below* may well find a really practical expression here. If we create the right balance of space and colour in our immediate home environment then this may assist our true inner or spiritual self to express its values and gifts or talents.

But what is a wonderfully comfortable or inspiring atmosphere for one individual may be an uncomfortable environment for another. Which is why it is so important to choose, decorate and arrange our own home for our own self.

If a home is shared with a partner, family or friends then it becomes much more difficult and some compromise is usually necessary unless everyone is fortunate enough to share very similar tastes and energies. Rather than compromise completely, it might be possible to keep one special space at home just for yourself. This is somewhere where your own personal energies can be recharged in a comfortable and auspicious environment. It could be just a small room or even part of the garden area, if this outdoor space is available.

So the choices we make in our home environment are important. Creating the right personal environment isn't always easy and many of us have lived in circumstances where we could only dream of a real home of our own and of what we would like to create around us there. Often it takes very little money simply to arrange what we have in an auspicious way.

Good use of colour can make all the difference with very little cost involved. When we consider that our personal home environment is one way of making a *connection* with our higher spiritual home so that we can bring a good strong and healthy energy flow between the two worlds, then the importance of our space becomes more obvious.

The clues to our higher spiritual home are not just found in the places where we live, there are echoes of this other reality in the way we move around from place to place.

The car has probably become the single biggest status symbol of our time. A recent conversation with a friend revealed that the type of car we choose can leave us open to speculation regarding our sexuality as well as our credit rating. The colour of the car that we choose matters too. All our colour choices reflect the vibrational levels which we feel attracted to or comfortable with, and each colour expresses particular qualities and energies. Given free choice, may of us would probably not have chosen the colour of car we are driving, as in the second-hand car market-place it is usually impossible to get everything we want altogether in one package. It is much easier to choose the colour we want if we are buying a brand new car. Although there is also the idea that we attract to ourselves exactly the energies – and colours – that we need at a particular time in our lives, so even if the colour of our vehicle may not have been our first choice, it could well be exactly right for us at this moment. It may be the colour/energy we need to bring into our life now.

The original word *ka* (not the twentieth century Ford manufacturer's name) was the Egyptian term used for our spiritual vehicle or our higher spiritual body or soul. The word car finds echoes of its earthly connection with the physical body in carnal, reincarnation, incarnate, carcass etc. The way the word is spelt is less important than the sound of the actual word. *It is the sound of the word that really matters.* Spelling and the written word are important in other ways, but the connections we are looking for are found mostly where they can be heard.

The ka is our spiritual body, our means of transportation on higher levels and the word now forms a physical link into our lives today. The way we use our motor car today is a poor substitute for the original free movement of our spiritual ka, which could traverse time and space.

The ancient memory of this ability still remains embedded deep inside our psyche, and so we try to recreate this freedom of movement and speed in our vehicles of today. Even our road system echoes the original subtle energy grid which still remains within our universe and planet. The original lines of communication for light, sound and the relocation of matter remain hidden to us, although there are vestiges of an ancient attempt to mark and map the system in our standing stones and dolmen found throughout the countryside.

Our highways and motorway network are another attempt to recreate what is already in existence on a higher level of consciousness.

The spiritual ka is a *light-body* — a body of light — and the pathways it uses to traverse this planet are known as light lines or leys. There are many interpretations of the word 'ley' which was first given to the world by Alfred Watkins in 1921 when he discovered that ancient monuments and sacred sites across the countryside were arranged in a pattern of straight lines which he called *leys*. The word ley can simply mean *line* or *straight line* but the word *leye* is also an obsolete Anglo-Saxon word for flame or fire. Lay or laid is similar in sound and means to deposit something, set it down or cause to lie, and lay-man is another term for an ordinary person.

Light and the concept of truth are always connected in spiritual understanding.

In order to tell a lie (untruth) it is necessary for one person to communicate with another, which means that there needs to be an exchange of information. Again, if we listen to the sounds of the words the connections can be made and understood. If we tell a lie then we create a false stream of words/information/understanding between ourselves and another person. We create a *lie* which is a very similar sound to the word *ley*, meaning light or line.

If the original leys were the lines of direct communication between individuals involved in the creation process and were based on *light* and *truth*, then to tell a lie is to create an artificial or false channel between each other. This lie then needs to be supported by our own energies because it cannot depend on the bright ley (light) energies of the universe.

It is why words spoken in truth somehow find support in the world around us, while words which are false eventually become faded or are somehow changed or exposed. Even clever lies seem to be un-enduring as time has a habit of exposing falsehood, whereas truth is already here. It is embedded in the light or ley system of the planet and our words and interchanges which are based in truth are supported by this system.

Remember that this is also the system which supports our *ka* or spiritual vehicle, therefore a life which is based on truth will help evolve a ka which is attracted to the true ley or light pathway system. The frequency or vibration will be compatible and therefore attractive.

A spiritual vehicle or ka which has not been enriched by the light of truth in its lifetime will find it more difficult to adapt to the high frequency of the lines of light, and for that individual the transition between death and the afterlife may be a rather prolonged and difficult period. The consequences of a lifetime based on false relationships and values will need to be expurgated. There is a similarity between the word *expurgate* and the idea of *purgatory* being, in some Christian traditions, the place for sinners (including those who lie) after death.

On a lighter note, *trains* are another interesting part of our transport system. The word itself can be translated as *t-rain*. The letter T is often used to represent the symbol of the cross and astrologically it represents this planet, Earth (the cross within the circle). So when T appears in a prominent position, such as the beginning of a word, then it can represent the earth i.e. Train = t-rain = earth-rain. There are other similar words which can be translated in this way like tread, trip, tear, time (again), town etc. With the word *train* comes the possible connection to water (rain) and the currents or rapid flows of water along particular pathways, often close to ley lines. It is a vague connection, but perhaps one worth mentioning.

Even the word *plane* itself suggests a higher level of existence or consciousness. The possibility of raising our own consciousness to a higher plane is accepted in some disciplines including yoga and meditation. The way we physically travel by plane also raises us high above the earth in a very physical way, giving a possible correspondence again between our physical and spiritual worlds.

The sea is another fascinating correlation. The words sea and see bring another dimension into this equation. It involves water again – with its hidden memory. To see also implies *to understand*. Perhaps our seas and oceans are really a huge depository of past knowledge which, once we have discovered the key to the memory in water, we can begin to unlock to reveal our true past inheritance.

We would then have a complete history (emotional as well as physical) of mankind and the planet Earth, the real earth-song, there for everyone to see – in the waters of the seas.

Conclusion

We are eternal beings. Our spiritual energies created the pattern or blueprint for life here on Earth and some of those once purely spiritual energies now remain here in physical human form. They relate on a subtle unconscious level and collectively their purpose is to further the evolution of the whole of humanity. Most often they are, as individuals, completely unaware of their own spiritual quest, simply feeling that the right thing to do is to pursue the search for truth in their own particular field or to support the expression of beauty and excellence in all forms of art, or to reinforce the need for peace and wisdom in all human endeavour. They are the *pillars of our human civilisations* and their existence is reflected in the standing stones, especially those in Stonehenge, Wiltshire, England.

These once purely spiritual beings formed the matrix upon which the whole of creation on this planet evolved and we can find clues to our creative origins in the patterns of life they produced which are all around us today. Everything we are is reflected into our environment, into the trees and the vegetation especially, and into the animal kingdom. The pictures in this book are only a few of the most obvious reflections. Once the pattern has been realised, it becomes easier to find other examples for ourselves.

Our connection with the mineral, vegetable and animal kingdoms on this planet means that our choices will always have a direct effect on these other levels of life. The genetic link is especially important because what we do in manipulating our own human genes will ultimately reflect through all the other levels of life, *and all of these levels will change in direct relationship to the human changes.* We need to be fully aware of our connection to the whole before we can safely experiment with genetic material because we are making changes, not just to ourselves, but ultimately for our whole planet and future. The long-term effect of our action needs to be more completely understood.

Homoeopathy provides us with a window through which we can glimpse one of the subtle mechanisms of connection between the levels of existence here.

Water is a substance which appears capable of recording our physical, emotional and mental energies and carrying this information – on the wind – into the other levels of life on this planet. The mineral, vegetable and animal kingdoms are – genetically and by means of the water we share – intrinsically linked to the human race. They are still dependent on their creative source, which is ourselves. The water contains an imprint of our past in physical, mental and emotional terms, and the wind carries that information into our future. The wind could, in this way, correspond to the *karmic airs* in Tibetan medicine. These airs circulate within the energy channels of the human body in a similar way to the winds that sweep across the earth.

The information transmitted in that way forms the connection between ourselves and the evolving environment and everything we are is carried on into the future of the planet. This is a necessary component for human survival as it also provides the impetus for plant growth and food production.

We will continue to struggle to control human issues such as the eating disorders which are now increasingly common in Europe and U.S.A. (compulsive eating leading to obesity and, at the other extreme, anorexia nervosa) until we understand the hidden mechanism behind the subtle means of human weight distribution. The mechanism is a complex one and this insight can only give just a glimpse of part of it, so that we might begin to imagine some of the issues involved.

We are linked together by a subtle energy network and the total amount of physical energy stored in our bodies has a real relationship to the number of human beings incarnate on this planet at any one time. Expressed simply, if people in some parts of the world continue to starve then others – who are unknowingly connected to them within the subtle energy web – will continue to gain weight by one means or another. They unknowingly also act as a conscience for all of us – the energies which surround the idea of conscience include those of blame and guilt.

Body weight is karmic in nature. The word *karma* means *action* and is essentially neutral in its expression – it does not necessarily mean *good* or *bad* action, simply *any* action of any kind. The energy required to carry out that action can be stored as body fat. Karma is the working out of the law of cause and effect and this can be an expression of group karma as well as individual karma. (The third law of physics states that for every action there must be an equal reaction.) So trying to treat obesity and slimming diseases on a purely physical level may not always be appropriate. There is much more for us to understand and a different perspective is urgently needed here. It might also include research into the ways in which the body stores different types of food as fat as there are also karmic relationships between the food/energy we take into our bodies and how we use/store that energy.

The words *meet* and *meat* have the same sounds and may also, in a spiritual sense have similar meanings. Also, the words *weight* and *wait* have the same energies within their sound and it could be that stored energy – weight – is *karma on-hold*, waiting to be discharged in appropriate action. Only action that is an appropriate balancing force will do to dissolve this karmic need and there may be many different reasons why the opportunity to use that stored energy has not presented itself at this time.

Then there is the relationship between soul groups. Sometimes physical energy may be stored by one individual because there are problems with energy flow and transmission within the group and it is not possible for those energies to be exchanged at that time. Or it may be that this particular individual carries the karmic weight or debt of the whole group or of particular members of the group. This can then leave others free to accomplish their particular piece of work. This is also an act of love.

Our current obsession with slimness and keeping fit is, in a strange way, an abdication of our responsibility – on a planetary level – to those who starve. We refuse to confront what these issues might mean on a global scale, preferring to concentrate our energies on the treadmill or the latest diet. We are trying – by artificial means – to control a mechanism which is ultimately there for our own protection. In doing so we have, inadvertently, shifted our collective responsibility on to those whose individual spiritual development (including their karmic and genetic inheritance) and position on the web makes it impossible for them to avoid weight gain. Even when they try, again and again, to lose the weight they carry, it is almost always regained – usually with a sense of intense failure and of inevitability. This is because what we are trying to challenge is something far greater and more complex than we have imagined, and it includes a planetary component which can be aligned against any individual personal attempt to change the situation.

When we lived in more isolated communities, without modern facilities for communication it would have been impossible to see the obvious connections between us globally.

Now that is changing and we are beginning to observe the real whole picture, and the best perspective we can have is when we take up our own position within it – as an individual, enduring, creative force here on Earth.

Our original spiritual level of existence or home reflects constantly on to our present physical universe. We can find markers pointing towards it in our everyday lives and within the English language, in simple words like car (ka), stone (s-tone) and electricity (el/elect-tri-city). All are important keys to the hidden mystery of ourselves and to the natural but hidden human initiatory experience.

As we descended, over millions of years, from a highly spiritual existence so our language descended from a highly intuitive and expressive musical level into the fragmented and broken version which is the speech we use today. Because we are now entering a time of rising spiritual energies which will eventually take us on the next loop of a spiral to a higher level of existence, our language is beginning to reveal glimpses of its spiritual origins. It is, in fact, *evolving for the first time* on an imaginary upward arch towards a more spiritual expression, after having descended over such a long period of time.

We take for granted the language we use every day, but if we can step back from it to examine it more closely other aspects of its organisation can start to emerge.

In his research into reverse speech, David John Oates of Reverse Speech Technologies suggests that the messages heard when music or speech is recorded and then played in reverse is a hidden communication of truth from the level of the collective unconscious, or perhaps the individual soul level. The reverse aspect can perhaps be attributed to the effect of a mirror image (of another higher level) which is reflected into our reality. To some extent, it can mean that we actually tell the truth even when we are lying because the reversed message will often tell a different story from the words that are being spoken at the time. In this way we can sometimes pick up – on an intuitive level – the fact that someone is telling less than the truth. The hidden message is heard and recognised by us and we just *know* that what is being said simply isn't true, even though there is nothing obviously inconsistent with the statement. This intuitive knowing is especially significant as the initial gradual opening of the heart centre occurs.

There are also clues in these pages which relate to the original system of subtle energy lines which were once more easily identified and used on this planet. This would have been when the frequency or vibrational level of existence here was considerably higher than today. It is this level which we are now moving towards once again. A system that has been hidden for thousands of years may well be on the verge of re-discovery. If, as these clues seem to suggest, it is connected with the transmission of energy and information, then it will transform the whole of the planetary energy system once again. It could finally release us from our dependence on fossil fuels and nuclear power, which are themselves an expression of lower or most dense energy levels. These changes will also come as a response to planetary need as the earth's resources are depleted.

Our own creative energies can help re-create what was once here, but only after we have understood our own inheritance and our own responsibility within the matrix. We are approaching a steep learning curve which, once scaled, has the potential to free us from the horrors of war, starvation and religious dogma forever.

In the meantime, we have something very simple yet extraordinarily important to learn. The time has arrived for us to know that the connections between ourselves are more than those of immediate family, distant relatives, partners, lovers, close friends and casual acquaintances. While it is true that for many of us these are our main lines of connection on the hidden energy web, there are those among us whose energy lines stretch much further afield – across cities, countries and continents, sometimes to the other side of the world. Most often these long-distance connections are sustained between the hidden network of global initiates whose work it is to serve humanity and to assist in human development and endeavour in whatever way possible. The opportunities which arise in the lives of these men and women will be taken and built upon to the best of their abilities, because it is in their spiritual nature to do so. They most often work in or around the energy centres of the planet which are usually, although not always, found in the major cities throughout the world.

These circles within the subtle planetary energy web are there also for the protection of everyone on the planet and their group energies constantly strive to balance the negative karmic influences which are always present in a (spiritually) evolving society.

It is important that these individuals acknowledge their own feelings of responsibility and caring, if only to themselves, because the links between them are important ones for everyone. If one of these connections begins to fail then it can affect the whole network, rather in the way a string of tiny decorative lights will fail to work if one bulb is broken or like a flowing stream of water when its natural course is suddenly artificially blocked or dammed, or, of course, *like one of the stone lintels or stone pillars falling within the circle*.

So the way that we care about each other as individuals is crucial, not least because it can affect the functioning of so many people spread across every continent. Paradoxically, it also protects our own life here, because once many of those who are our immediate neighbours on the web have passed on from physical incarnation, our position here becomes untenable and our time to leave this physical incarnation comes. No-one is immune or can stand alone, as every human being is part of a group of other human beings, all connected by fine lines of light on higher soul-energy levels.

Our connections within this subtle web are not always compatible or easy ones. Often an opposing (or balancing) energy is needed to balance the network or to teach us something important which will ultimately assist us in individual and group development. Or sometimes this balancing role will fall to ourselves for the same reason, perhaps to assist unconsciously another in our group to become certain of their own decisions and intuitive choices. At the time, these influences will be experienced as hurtful or disturbing, often to an extent far beyond anything we would expect to experience. This is because when one of our soul group is at odds with the rest of the group it produces great disturbance on a spiritual level and is felt to some extent throughout the whole group, although it is experienced most acutely by those closest to that particular individual on the network. The person closest to us spiritually on the network may be at the other side of the world – unknown to us individually – someone whose life and environment may be completely different to our own. The feelings that we experience also will be accepted and interpreted as belonging to our own personal experience and our own immediate environment.

Our spiritual brother or sister may or may not be a member of our immediate family, but instead may be someone who has been connected to us for many incarnations, someone who we may or may not have met in this lifetime. The connection remains always because it is love-based and real – unconditional – love is one of the qualities of eternity.

In writing these pages I have been keenly aware of the process involved in bringing any previously hidden, esoteric knowledge into the public arena. Whenever I have hesitated in writing about some particular aspect of that knowledge I have felt an almost physical push, closely followed by an overwhelming need to include a particular piece of text.

In discussing the hidden meaning of Stonehenge in particular, I have often hesitated and there has been much soul searching on my part regarding the inclusion of this insight. The title of the book 'The Virgin Stones' was inspired by that particular chapter and as this title was intuitively given to me many years later while I was doing other related research, I have decided to let it be.

When these insights first arrived with me, I had absolutely no framework in which to place them. I was an ordinary housewife, living a suburban lifestyle on the outskirts of Manchester and my understanding of metaphysics or of anything connected with occult knowledge was practically non-existent.

This journey has embraced a very steep learning curve,

prompted by an overwhelming need to find the right way of expressing this information. I felt strongly at the time of the experiences in 1984 that whatever I did to facilitate bringing this information into the public arena, I should try to keep the insights themselves as intact and fresh as possible. While I have consistently born this in mind, it is inevitable that ideas and writings from other people have coloured the view. Often these impressions and ideas have not been actively sought by myself, but seem to have arrived with me in many different ways often exactly at the time they were most needed, like carefully chosen gifts. For this process I will always be grateful and if I have overlooked to acknowledge any author or other contact whose contribution is here then I apologise sincerely for my oversight.

As far as I'm aware what is given here has not been revealed in this way until now. It was a great privilege to work with this material and my hope is that it will be considered with an open mind and – more importantly – intuitively recognised by an open heart.

Notes

The Human Energy-body & The Chakras

We are spiritual beings who are at this time experiencing life in a physical environment. Our understanding of who and what we are is temporarily restricted by the comparatively narrow perspective of our own five senses.

Metaphysics is a strange animal. Basic metaphysics can be the tool which allows us to explore the possibilities of E.S.P., clairvoyance, alternative methods of healing and similar subject areas. It is the ancient hidden science behind the healing needles of acupuncture and, more recently, has been the basis of homoeopathic techniques and many other alternative healing treatments, including aromatherapy and reflexology. It is the tool that helps us to explore the possibilities of the subtle human energy body and to begin to understand the qualities of the hidden energy centres known as the *chakras*.

The human energy-body is a dynamic, vibrant energy field which permeates the whole of our physical existence. Within this intensely fluctuating field of subtle energies are some significant developmental centres known as the chakras.

The seven energy centres illustrated here are the best known chakra centres, but there are many more. They are linked by *nadis* (subtle energy threads) to the spinal channel which is the pathway for the *kundalini* energy flow.

Kundalini is the fiery energy of life and is understood to coil – like a serpent – at the base of the spine in the subtle energy body of the human being. It rises up the three subtle energy channels which run alongside the spinal column (Ida, Pingala and Sushumna).

Each of the chakras also links, through the physical endocrine system, to one of the ductless glands i.e. adrenal, thyroid, pineal etc.

There are energy channels, also known in Chinese medicine as *meridians*, which conduct the flow of subtle energies throughout the human energy body. These can be stimulated at certain points by the needles of acupuncture or by acupressure. Sometimes moxibustion (the appliance of heat) is used to facilitate the energy flow at certain points along these lines.

The energy centres – chakras – evolve within the human subtle energy body over many thousands of years and rarely function to their full capacity in any individual at this present time. The centres themselves are all at different stages of development in the subtle energy body of each individual and will evolve in accordance with the experiences that particular spiritual being encounters over very great periods of time.

Most of us now have fully functioning energy centres in the subtle energy body below the diaphragm, and at the present time most of us are unconsciously focussing our spiritual development on the energy centre at the throat, connecting to the thyroid gland in our physical body. This gland is especially significant in balancing the metabolism, which in turn is relevant in controlling body weight. This energy centre is concerned with intellect and communication and is currently expressed through our use of language, music, writing and information technology.

The Chakras

Only the seven major chakras or subtle energy centres are discussed here. There are many more. Each chakra has an original Sanskrit name and each relates to specific endocrine glands within the physical body. The configuration is shown below:

CHAKRA	SANSKRIT NAME	ENDOCRINE GLAND
Base	*Muludhara*	Adrenal or suprarenal
Sacral	*Svadhistana*	Reproductive organs
Solar Plexus	*Manipura*	Pancreas
Heart	*Anahata*	Thymus
Throat	*Vishudda*	Thyroid
Brow	*Ajna*	Pituitary
Crown	*Sahasrara*	Pineal

Each centre relates to a different stage in human evolution, beginning with the Base centre which is primal, tribal and focusses on the initial generative energies of creation.

THE SACRAL centre is creative in a different way and its energy provides the impetus for sexual activity as well as other creative energies.

THE SOLAR PLEXUS focusses the development of emotional energies and encourages their exchange.

THE HEART is the centre of the intuition and of higher spiritual love. It is also the seat of the conscience.

THE THROAT centre focusses on verbal and intellectual expression and communication.

THE BROW centre brings together the energies of the Heart and those of the Throat centres. It is the centre of deeper understanding and vision.

THE CROWN centre combines all of these centres and brings them together in an explosion of universal (unconditional) love and wisdom.

Evolutionary subtle energies are transmitted through the chakra system in a particular way (please see illustration). The kundalini energy flow gradually rises (over many thousands of years) from the base centre to the crown centre, from the sacral centre to the thyroid centre, from the solar plexus centre to the heart centre and from the heart and thyroid centres to the brow centre (via alta-major centre at the back of the head). For most human beings this is a slow, gradual process which takes many millions of years. During the human initiatory process this time-scale is considerably shortened.

The present position in development for most individuals is centred on the Throat centre and, consequently, the next energy centre to gradually develop, over many thousands of years, will be the Heart centre. To a certain extent, energy centres may be open and operating within the subtle energy body, but without being in any way *fully developed* and functioning properly. Their developmental stage will always depend on the spiritual evolution of the individual concerned.

CHAKRAS

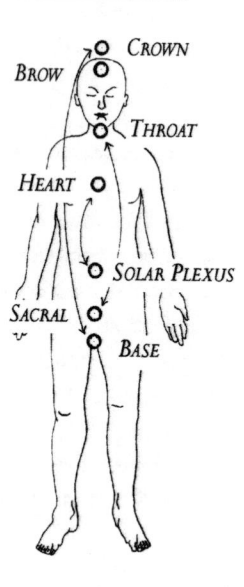

The kundalini energy flow gradually rises (over many thousands of years) from the base centre to the crown centre, from the sacral centre to the thyroid centre, from the solar plexus centre to the heart centre and from the heart and thyroid centres to the brow centre (via alta-major centre at the back of the head). All these energies will eventually rise to the crown centre. For most human beings this is a slow, gradual process which takes many millions of years. During the human initiatory process this time-scale is considerably shortened.

The Planetary Energy-Body

The energy-body which surrounds and permeates the planet itself is not dissimilar to the human energy body described above. This is also a dynamic, pulsating and fluctuating field which affects our climate and weather systems. Everything we experience on this dense physical level is also experienced on higher energy levels, within the subtle energy body of Gaia.

Some of the significant energy centres or chakras described above relate – on a physical level – to our larger towns and cities. Others are in less densely populated places such as Stonehenge in Wiltshire and Glastonbury. All of these places are important in planetary terms and what happens in them can affect the whole global subtle energy field.

The illustration shows how the thinning of the ozone layer is also reflected in the subtle energy field of the planet itself. This hole may have its origin in the subtle energy body because the likelihood is that dis-ease begins on higher levels than the physical. What we may be experiencing on a global level in the thinning of the ozone layer would have been apparent much earlier in the thinning of the subtle energy body, had we had the means to detect it.

The time-span involved is important. It takes much longer – perhaps several decades – for events such as nuclear explosion, pollution or de-forestation to impact on a global level. The effects we see today have causes that were generated many years ago.

GLOSSARY

ACUPUNCTURE
Ancient system of Chinese medicine in which a trained practitioner will insert needles on particular points in the physical body which correspond to known points in the subtle energy body, usually along the meridians or energy channels.

ACUPRESSURE
Method used to stimulate the subtle energy points by applying pressure to them, usually by using the hands or feet.

ALTA MAJOR CENTRE
Hidden chakra or subtle energy centre situated at the back of the head between the throat centre and the brow centre. Acts as transformer for rising kundalini energies.

AURA
Word traditionally used to describe the subtle energy body as it appears to surround the individual. Sanskrit = 'vital air or breath'.

BASE CENTRE
First chakra (muludhara) or lowest subtle energy centre. Please see notes on chakras.

BROW CENTRE
Sixth chakra (ajna) or subtle energy centre. Please see notes on chakras.

CHAKRA
Subtle energy centre – please see notes. Sanskrit = *wheel*.

CHI
Subtle vital energy connected with sunlight. Especially strong when close to water or where earth and water meet such as at the seaside, lakeside or on the riverbank. This is the energy which flows through the subtle energy body.

CROWN CENTRE
Seventh chakra (sahasrara) or subtle energy centre. Please see notes on the chakras.

FENG SHUI
Wind & water. The Chinese art of placement or *geomancy*.

GAIA
The earth spirit, traditionally felt to be female.

GEOMANCY
Chinese traditional art of placement, also known as *Feng Shui*.

HEART CENTRE
Fourth chakra or subtle energy centre (anahata). Please see notes.

HALO
Burst of subtle energy surrounding the head of an individual, originating from the crown chakra.

HOMOEOPATHY
Homoeopathic medicine relies on the premise that *like cures like* and uses substances known to produce a similar effect to the disease they are meant to cure. These substances are diluted in water so as to leave no physical trace of their existence in the water itself. Only the *memory pattern* of the substance remains.

INITIATE
Used here to indicate someone who has undergone a series of physical/emotional/mental and spiritual trials which enable them to compress the total human learning experience (of many lifetimes) into a much shorter period.

INITIATION
Used here to illustrate the process and meaning of above. Not to be confused with the initiation ceremonies of some groups and societies.

KARMA
Simply means *action*. Used here to indicate the spiritual law of cause and effect. Karma can be *individual*, *inherited* (family), *group* (usually soul-group) or what used to be termed *tribal* but now most likely to be expressed *nationally* or even *globally*.

KARMIC WINDS
Known in Tibetan medicine and used here to describe the flow of subtle energy throughout the body.

KUNDALINI
The fiery energy of creation. Traditionally thought to curl – like a snake – within the base centre or chakra at the base of the spinal column. Kundalini rises naturally as part of the evolutionary process but its progression is quickened during the initiation process. Probably the human equivalent of atomic energy on a planetary scale.

LEY
The word ley can simply mean *line* or *straight line* and *leye* is also an obsolete Anglo-Saxon word for flame or fire.

MERIDIANS
Energy channels (within the subtle energy body) used in acupuncture and Chinese medicine. Please see illustration.

MOXIBUSTION
Application of heat (usually burning herb) to acupuncture points.

NADIS
Subtle energy strands or threads within the energy body.

OCCULT
Hidden. The word is used here only to describe *hidden knowledge*, usually of a metaphysical nature.

PRANA
See *Chi*.

REIKI
System of spiritual healing based around subtle energy body work.

SAAMI / SAMI
Indigenous peoples of arctic region especially northern Europe and Russia. Traditionally associated with reindeer herding in Lapland.

SACRAL CENTRE
Second chakra (svadhistana) or subtle energy centre. Relating to light. Sacr = light, also as in sacred. Please see notes.

SHAMAN
Spiritual leader and healer often relying on ecstatic trance and musical ritual associated with drumming. Traditionally an hereditary position within the tribe or group, although the call to shamanic practice may come without this family connection.

SOLAR PLEXUS CENTRE
Third chakra (manipura) or subtle energy centre. Please see notes.

SUBTLE ENERGY BODY
Vibrant hidden energy field surrounding and interpenetrating all life. Notes describe human subtle energy body and the global subtle energy body in more detail.

THROAT CENTRE
Fifth chakra (vishudda) or subtle energy centre. Please see notes.

THERAPEUTIC TOUCH
System of spiritual healing closely associated with the channelling of subtle energy, most often through the hands.

VIRGIN
Pure. Used in this context to describe particular individuals who are born completely free of any karmic inheritance of their own from past lives. Their individual karma is often resolved within each lifetime and this makes it possible for them to take on or carry the karmic inheritance of others.

Bibliography

Bailey A.A. (1922) *Initiation, Human & Solar*, Lucifer Publishing Co (Lucis Trust)

Baker D.B. Dr. (1975) *The Jewel in the Lotus*, Douglas Baker Pub.

Baker D.B. Dr. (1975) *Meditation – The Theory & Practice*, Douglas Baker Pub.

Besant A. & Leadbeater C (First pub. 1908). *Occult Chemistry*, Theosophical Publishing House

Blavatsky H.P. (1888) *The Secret Doctrine*, Theosophical Publishing House

Bloom W. (1996) *Money, Heart & Mind*, Arkana/Penguin

Brennan B.A. (1993) *Light Emerging*, Bantam Books

Clifford T. (1984) *Tibetan Buddhist Medicine & Psychiatry – The Diamond Healing*, Aquarian

Devereux P. (2001) *Stone Age Soundtracks*, Vega

Devereux P. (1991) *Earth Memory*, Quantum

Gerber R. M.D. (1988) *Vibrational Medicine*, Bear & Co.

Hall D. (1994) *Iridology*, Piatkus

Heath R. (1999) *Stone Circles – A Beginner's Guide*, Hodder & Stoughton

Hoffstein R.M. (1992) *A Mystical Key to the English Language*, Destiny Books

Kaptchuk T.J. (1983) *Chinese Medicine*, Rider

Lansdowne Z.F. (1990) *Rules for Spiritual Initiation*, Samuel Weiser

Lawson-Wood D. & J. (1974) *The Incredible Healing Needles*, Samuel Weiser

Leadbeater C.W. (1927) *The Chakras*, Quest – Theosophical Publishing House

Moyne E.J. (1981) *Raising the Wind – The legend of Lapland and Finland Wizards in Literature*, Assoc. University Presses, Inc.

Myers N. (1985) *The Gaia Atlas of Planet Management*, Pan Books

Newall R.S. (1959) *Stonehenge*, H.M.S.O.

Roney-Dougal S. (1991) *Where Science & Magic Meet*, Element

Skinner S. (1989) *The Living Earth Manual of Feng Shui*, Arkana/Penguin

Schiff M. (1995) *The Memory of Water*, Thorsons

Schlemmer P.V. & Jenkins P. (1993) *The Only Planet of Choice*, Gateway

Vithoulkas G. (1980) *The Science of Homoeopathy*, Thorsons

ABOUT THE AUTHOR

Joyce's interest in personal and planetary awareness, human spirituality and metaphysics has now spanned many years and began as a result of a series of profound spiritual experiences in 1984. Her subsequent studies in metaphysics with Claregate College in London were followed by a period of research and retreat at the Krotona Institute in California. She spent some time in northern Finland where her focus on Shamanism and Healing in the North helped to gain her Diploma in Arctic Studies from the University of Lapland, as well as her B.A. (Hons) Independent Study degree in Manchester.

She has run workshops and courses, including 'Exploring the Unexplained' at Manchester University and is committed to bringing esoteric knowledge into an arena where it can be examined and discussed openly. She is about to embark on part-time research for her Ph.D. with the Open University.

Her wish is to build a centre for related research, teaching and healing in Manchester, England.

Permission

Grateful thanks to The Theosophical Publishing House, Adyar, Chennai 600 020, India for permission to reproduce Fig. 47 – Ozone and the first paragraph of description on ozone on page 96 of their book *Occult Chemistry* by Annie Besant and C.W. Leadbeater.

Apologies & Thanks

I tried very hard to have this book printed on recycled paper. The cost was almost double that for non-recycled paper and proved much too expensive. I hope that some day soon we will be using recycled products as a matter of course and that with increasing demand the costs will become less.

My thanks to Temple Design for all their help in getting quotations for recycled products and for finding paper from a sustainable source for the printing, and also for their skills and assistance in publishing this book.